NETWORKING
MADE EASY

Get Yourself Connected

By James Bernstein

10 9 8 7 6 5 4 3 2 1

Contents

Introduction

These days everyone is connected to everyone else via their desktop, laptop, smartphone, gaming system, and so on. They use these devices go online, send emails, share files, and more. And with so much information out there to be shared, we need to have a reliable network in the background allowing all that data to flow smoothly.

Computer networking has been around almost as long as the computer itself. But these days it's way more advanced than back in the beginning when it was just a few computers in one centralized building or even in the same room. And there is much more involved technology-wise to keep everything communicating reliably and with the speed required to keep everyone happy.

This goal of this book is to help you increase your knowledge of how today's modern networks operate and the hardware and software that is needed to make it all work. I will discuss the basics and tell you what you need to know to get your network up and running, and also go into more advanced topics such as routing protocols so you can see that there is much more to networking than you might think. I'm not going to make things too complicated, since the purpose of this book is to increase your networking knowledge without making you want to give up on the subject entirely.

So, on that note, let's get things started and turn you into a networking expert—or at least get you a few steps closer!

Chapter 1 – What is a Network?

Let's begin our networking journey with a discussion of what exactly a network *is*. A network is a system of computers and other devices that are connected together via cabling or wirelessly for the purpose of sharing resources, data, and applications. Network design can vary from a simple network of two computers connected together to a vast network spanning multiple locations and even across continents (such as the Internet).

Peer to Peer vs. Client-Server Networks
There are two main types of networks that you should know about, and they each serve a similar purpose but are configured and managed differently.

Peer to peer networks (also called workgroups) were the first type of network to be used. In this type of network, there is no centralized management or security and each computer is in charge of its own local users and file and folder permissions. Since there is no centralized user management, any user who wants access to resources on another computer will need to have an account on that specific computer. So, if a user wants access to files on ten different computers, then that user will need ten separate user accounts. Computers on a peer to peer network are usually connected together through a simple hub or network switch (figure 1.1).

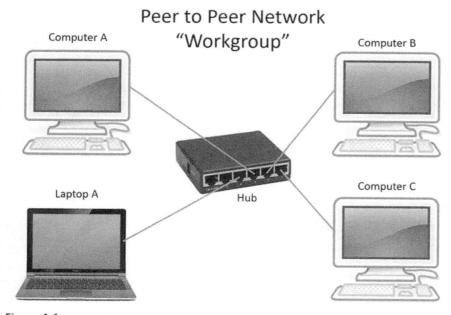

Figure 1.1

So, if Sally is a user on Computer A and she wants to access files on Laptop A and Computer C, then an admin on Laptop A and Computer C will need to make a user account for her and then assign the permissions she needs to be able to access those resources. You can imagine how complicated this would get as the number of computers on the network grows.

When the number of computers in a peer to peer network starts to go past ten, then you can run into problems such as slowdowns from network broadcasts and other traffic because all the traffic goes to each computer even though only the computer that it was meant to go to will accept the information. Plus, many workgroup configured operating systems can only accept ten concurrent connections at a time. So, if you have a computer acting as a file server for twenty users, then only ten of them can connect to that file server at a time.

Peer to peer networks work fine for home networks or small office networks where there are not a lot of users and computers to manage. But once you get to a certain limit, that is where you need to implement something more, such as a client-server network.

A client-server network has clients (workstations) as well as a server (or many servers). As you can see in figure 1.2, the clients are labeled Computer A, Computer B, Laptop A, and so on. There is also a file server and a directory server, which is used to manage user accounts and access controls.

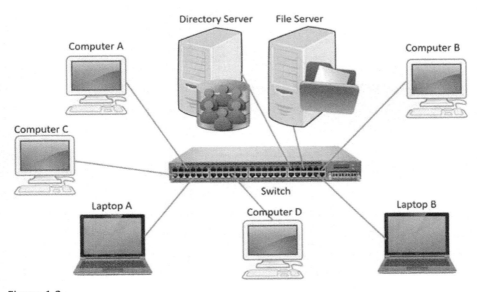

Figure 1.2

All the computers and servers connect to each other via a network switch rather than a hub like we saw in the peer to peer network, even though you can use a switch for a peer to peer network as well. The main advantage here is that every user account is created on the directory server, and then each computer, laptop, and other servers are joined to a domain where authentication is centralized for logins and resource permissions. A domain is a centralized way to manage computers, users, and resources, and each computer joins the domain and each user is created as a domain user. So, if a user named Joe on computer C wants to access files on Laptop B, they can do so assuming their user account is allowed to. There is no need to make a user account for Joe on Laptop B or any other computer on the network besides the initial user created on the directory server.

Using a switch rather than a hub reduces broadcast traffic because the switch knows what port each computer is connected to and doesn't have to go to each computer or server to find the one it is trying to get to. Switches can be thought of as "smart" hubs, or hubs can be thought of as "dumb" switches.

The client-server model is also very scalable, and the amount of concurrent connections to a server is only limited to the licensing model in place and eventually the hardware limits in regards to network bandwidth and server capacity. Directory servers can handle managing thousands of users with little hardware resources needed.

The downsides of the client-server model include:

- Increased costs because servers are more expensive than computers and network switches are more expensive than hubs.
- More difficult to implement and maintain because of its complexity.
- Single point of failure if a directory server goes down and none of your users can log in. This is often bypassed by having multiple directory servers (or domain controllers).

Overall, if your environment has many resources and you want to centralize management of your users and computers, then you should go with the client-server model. If you only have a few computers and users, then a peer to peer configuration should work just fine. Plus, you can reconfigure it to a client-server model in the future if needed.

Network Devices

When many people start learning about networking, they assume that a network only consists of computers talking to each other. In some cases this is true, like in many small peer to peer home networks, but in the real world there is usually much more to it.

Network devices can consist of many things, including:
- Computers
- Servers
- Printers
- Copiers
- Storage arrays
- Wireless access points\Wi-Fi routers

Of course, there are also routers, switches, and firewalls (which I will discuss in Chapter 2).

You can even consider your smartphone and tablet as network devices because they are technically on your network and are connected to your wireless access point to get their Internet connection. You will probably hear me say this many times in this book, but the Internet is the biggest network in the world.

Network Terminology

There is a lot of terminology that goes along with networking, as well as acronyms for just about everything. I will be going over many of them in this book, but for now I wanted to talk about some of the more common terms that you might have heard of. Then we will get into the more complicated (and exciting) stuff later. Many of these terms will be discussed later on, so I won't go into too much detail just yet.

- **Ethernet** – A standard of network communication using twisted pair cable.
- **Server** – A computer (or other device) that is used to store files or host an application.
- **Bandwidth** – The capacity of a network communications link to transmit the maximum amount of data it can from one point to another over a network connection.
- **Fiber Optic** – A type of network cable that uses a super thin glass or plastic core to transmit data via a light signal.
- **Network Card** – A piece of hardware installed in a computer or other device that is used to transmit network data from the network to the device itself.
- **Protocol** – A set of rules used in network communication between devices needed to exchange information correctly.

- **Packet** – A small amount of data sent over a network that contains information such as the source and destination address as well as the information that is meant to be transmitted.
- **Port** – A number that identifies one side of a connection between two computers that is used to identify a specific process.
- **IP Address** – A 32 bit binary number used to identify network devices on a network.
- **ISP** – An Internet Service Provider is the company you get your Internet connection from.
- **Cat5 Cable** – Category 5 cabling is a standard of network cable that is of a certain type and speed rating. Cat5 is considered to be outdated these days, and has been replaced by faster versions such as Cat6 and Cat7.
- **Host** – A device on a network. Usually a computer or server.
- **LAN** – A Local Area Network is a network contained within one building.
- **DNS** – The Domain Naming System translates hostnames to their IP addresses so we don't need to remember IP addresses when connecting to other network devices.
- **DHCP** – The Dynamic Host Configuration Protocol is used to assign IP address to devices so they are able to communicate on the network.

Network Speeds

When it comes to network hardware, not all network devices are equal when it comes to speed. And when it comes to network performance, speed costs money. Network speeds have been increasing over the years, and these faster devices are becoming more commonplace, so you will see them being used more often.

Network speeds are usually measured in Mbps (Megabits per second) and Gbps (Gigabits per second) with 1Gbps equal to 1000Mbps. Back in the beginning days of networking, speeds were around 10Mbps. Now it's common to see 10Gbps and even 40Gbps being used in modern datacenters.

In order for a network to be able to utilize the desired speed, the hardware and the cabling need to be able to support that particular speed, otherwise the network will function at the speed of the slowest device on the link. That doesn't mean that if you have five computers with 10Gbps network cards and one with a 10Mbps network card that all the computers will function at 10Mbps. It will depend on the network configuration itself.

When it comes to Ethernet cables, make sure you use at least Category 5e cabling so you can get 1Gbps speeds out of your network. If possible, skip Cat 5e and go for Cat 6.

OSI Model

Now it's time for a little networking theory (I know you're excited for this!). If you plan on having a career in the networking field, then you will need to know about the Open Systems Interconnection reference model. The OSI model was developed in the 1970s by the International Organization for Standardization (ISO) to help standardize network technologies so computers from different manufacturers could communicate with each other by making compatible network hardware, software, and protocols.

The OSI Model is divided up into seven layers or logical groupings that are grouped in a hierarchical format. I will briefly go over each layer and its purpose next. If you want to turn yourself into a super networking geek, then you should go out and find some resources that cover the OSI Model in greater detail.

- **Application Layer** – This is where users communicate and interact with the computer and use programs (applications).
- **Presentation Layer** – This layer presents data to the Application layer and translates the data as needed.
- **Session Layer** – Here is where network sessions between the Presentation layer entries are set up, managed, and dismantled.
- **Transport Layer** – This layer takes data from the upper layers and combines it into a data stream providing end to end data transport services.
- **Network Layer** – Also known as layer 3, this is where device addressing and data tracking takes place.
- **Data Link Layer** – Provides for the physical transmission of data and also takes care of flow control and error notifications.
- **Physical Layer** – This layer communicates with the actual communication media using bits which have a value of either 0 or 1.

Packets, Frames, and Headers

Now that we know that networking involves transmitting data between two or more devices along a network media such as a cable (or at least we should know), let's now take a look at the actual data that is formatted on its journey.

Packets
A network packet (also called a datagram) is a formatted unit of data that not only has the information that is meant to be sent to its destination (the payload) but also contains control information such as the source and destination address that is used to make sure the payload arrives where it was meant to go. Networks that use packets to send data are called packet switched networks at the Network Layer (layer 3). Think of packets as chunks of data sent over the network so that congestion doesn't take place because of too much traffic on the media.

A packet is created by the sending device and then is sent to the protocol stack running on that device, where it is then sent out on the network via the networking hardware. Then on the receiving end the packet is passed to the appropriate protocol stack and processed. There are some other things that take place within this process as the packet traverses the OSI layers, but for the sake of keeping it simple, let's just say a packet goes from the source device to the destination device over the network and contains the data that is meant to be delivered along with other data that help move the process along.

Figure 1.3 shows the most basic form of a packet and includes the source address, destination address, type (tells the OS what kind of data the frame carries), the data, and then CRC information. CRC stands for cyclic redundancy check, and it performs error checking functions. There are other types of packets but we will mostly be concerned with IP packets for our discussion.

Source Address	Destination Address	Type	Data	CRC

Figure 1.3

Frames
Frames are also considered to be a unit of data themselves, and operate at the Data Link layer (layer 2). They are very similar to packets in the way the work is constructed, but their structure is different. Frames are used to transport data on the same network and use source and destination MAC addresses (discussed in Chapter 5) rather than IP addresses. A frame is sent over the network and an Ethernet switch checks the destination address of the frame against a MAC lookup table in its memory. Then, it takes that information to determine which port to send the data out so it reaches its intended destination. Figure 1.4 shows the components of a typical network frame.

Preamble	SFD	Destination MAC Address	Source MAC Address	Type	Data and Padding	FCS

Figure 1.4

Preamble – An alternating 1,0 patter that tells the receiving system that a frame is starting and enables synchronization.

- **SFD (Start Frame Delimiter)** – Denotes that the destination MAC Address field begins with the next byte.
- **Destination MAC Address** – The address of the receiving device.
- **Source MAC Address** – The address of the source device.
- **Type** – Identifies the Network Layer protocol used.
- **Data and Padding** – Contains the payload data sent down from the Data Link Layer to the Network Layer. Padding data is added to meet the minimum length requirement for this field, and can be 46 to 1500 bytes.
- **FCS (Frame Check Sequence)** – The field at the end of the frame that contains a Cyclic Redundancy Check (CRC) which allows for the detection of corrupted data.

Headers

Headers are used as part of the process of packaging of data for transfer over network connections. There are two types of headers, and they are TCP and UDP (TCP and UDP are discussed in Chapter 6). TCP headers contain 20 bytes while UDP headers contain 8 bytes.

Think of a header as information that helps prepare an end device for additional, more specific information. A header contains addressing and other data that is required for a packet to reach its intended destination. So, without a header, your data won't make it to where you want it to go.

A header can contain the following information:

- The version of IP (IPv4 or IPv6)
- The sender's IP address
- The receiver's IP address
- The number of packets in the message
- The protocol being used
- The time to live
- The packet length (if applicable)
- Synchronization data

Collision and Broadcast Domains

Just like a freeway can get crowded with cars, a network can get crowded with its own type of traffic and cause performance issues and the potential for lost data. When traffic is flowing smoothly, then everything is great. But when you have traffic collisions and too much data being sent over the media on your network, that's when things can get messy. In the networking world there are terms to describe these scenarios, and they are collision domains and broadcast domains.

Collision Domain

A collision domain is a term used to describe a group of networked devices on a network segment where one of those devices sends out a packet on the segment and all of the other devices on that segment are forced to pay attention to it. But if another device sends out a packet at the same time, then you will have a collision, which will require the packet to be resent.

Back in the old days of hubs, if one computer sent out a packet, then every other computer connected to that hub or even to other hubs on that segment would be forced to listen to the transmission. Collisions would occur if more than one device transmitted at the same time. Today's switches help alleviate collisions by making each port its own collision domain, greatly reducing the amount of collisions. These days collisions are also greatly reduced by using full duplex connections, where the network devices are able to send and receive at the same time.

Broadcast Domain

A broadcast domain is a term used to describe a group of networked devices on a network that hears all broadcasts that have been sent on all segments. A broadcast is where a device sends out a message to every device on the network. This is another reason we use switches instead of hubs, to reduce the size of our broadcast domains and prevent broadcast storms.

As you can see in figure 1.5, we have two networks connected to our router by switches. Each port on the switch connects to a computer and is considered a collision domain. Then all of the computers connected to that switch are part of a broadcast domain. Routers won't pass broadcast traffic, so we don't need to worry about the computers on Network 2 getting broadcast traffic from Network 1.

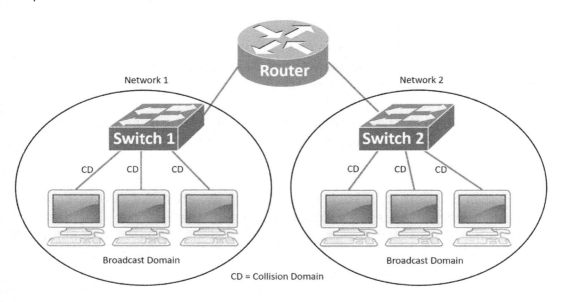

Figure 1.5

LAN vs. WAN

If you've done any type of networking or IT work, then you will most likely have heard the term Local Area Network (or LAN) and maybe even Wide Area Network (or WAN). But what is the difference between the two? Well, I'm glad you asked!

A LAN is a network that spans one location such as your home, office, or even an entire building. Some people also consider networks that span a location like a school campus a LAN. The network devices can be connected via cabling or by using a wireless connection. The network may consist of one network segment or multiple network segments with different IP address ranges assigned to them. To use different IP address ranges on a network requires the use of a layer 3 device like a router or layer 3 switch to allow the segments to communicate with each other. (IP addresses will be discussed in Chapter 5 and routers and switches will be discussed in Chapter 2.)

A WAN, on the other hand, is a network that extends over a large geographical distance such as between cities, states, or even countries. Since it's not possible to use standard networking media such as Ethernet cables or Wi-Fi connections, WANs rely more on leased lines from entities like phone companies and cable providers to cover the larger distances. These connections usually consist of long fiber optic cable runs designed for long distance communications.

Chapter 2 – Networking Hardware

One of the key elements to having a reliable network is to get the best hardware you can buy, since just like with everything else in this world, you get what you pay for! There are several networking components that are needed to build a functioning network, and then there are other components that are more of an option.

Network Adapter

Let's start this discussion with one of the most basic (and cheapest) components, which would be the network adapter (figure 2.1). Network adapters are used as the interface between the network and the computer, server, printer, or whatever device that the adapter is installed in. A computer (etc.) can have several network adapters, and network adapters can come with several network ports on one adapter. Common ports for these adapters include RJ45, which is used for Ethernet cables, and SFP, SC, LC, and GBIC connections for fiber optic cables. The cable connects to the port on the back of the card and then the card itself plugs into a slot on the motherboard in the computer.

Figure 2.1

Many desktop computers have built-in network adapters that are integrated with the motherboard similar to the way laptops are designed. This doesn't mean that you can't upgrade your network adapter with a faster model or one with more ports.

Always make sure you have the appropriate slot type free on your motherboard before you decide to upgrade your network card or add a standalone model so you don't have to make another trip to the store!

Hub

Next I want to briefly mention a network device that is pretty much obsolete, but you might run into one of them at some point in your networking career. Hubs (figure 2.2) are devices with four or more ports (usually not more than sixteen ports) that simply transfer the packets from the network cable out all the ports. Hubs are layer 1 devices and also act as repeaters, meaning they regenerate the signal, allowing it to travel further down the cable than it would if it was just a straight cable run.

Figure 2.2

The problem with hubs is that they are "dumb", meaning they don't know anything about any of the devices on the network and that's why they just forward all the traffic out all the ports, which is also known as broadcasting. This is why they are not practical on larger networks and usually only seen on small home networks.

If you ever encounter a situation where someone is using a hub on their home or small office network, feel free to replace it with even a cheap switch to improve performance.

Switch

Network switches (figure 2.3) are what we use instead of hubs when we want to build a network the right way. Switches have built-in intelligence, and some more so than others. Switches operate at layer 2, and can also operate at layer 3 assuming you have the right type. Layer 3 switches can also perform routing like a router does (discussed next).

Figure 2.3

The way a switch functions is by keeping track of the MAC addresses of devices that pass traffic through it. MAC addresses are the burned in hardware address that every network device has, and will be discussed in more detail in Chapter 5. This MAC address information is stored in MAC filter tables (also known as Content Addressable Memory tables).

By referencing these tables they avoid broadcasting all network traffic out all ports whenever some device on the network decides it wants to start communicating. Once a MAC address is stored on the switch with its associated\connected port number, the switch will only pass traffic through that port when traffic comes into the switch for a device with a known MAC address. One downside is when the switch is powered off the information on the MAC filter table is lost and it has to be rebuilt, as connections are made after the switch is turned back on.

Router

At layer 3 of the OSI Model we have routers, which perform a variety of functions to keep data flowing on the network. The purpose of a router (figure 2.4) is to "route" traffic from one network to the other. If you want to communicate with a computer or other device on a network that is different from your own, then the traffic will need to be routed between them.

Routers use IP addresses to forward traffic while switches rely on MAC addresses to take care of their traffic. Layer 3 switches can also route traffic between different networks while also performing switching functions. They are not a replacement for routers, but are instead used internally for different network segments within your organization.

When some data (network packet) comes in on one of the ports on the router, the router reads the network address information in the packet to determine its destination. Then, using information in its routing table or policy, it sends the packet to the next network to ultimately get to its final destination. It might have to go through several routers (with each step called a hop) to get to its destination.

Routing tables are databases stored in RAM that contain information about directly connected networks. These tables can be updated and maintained dynamically (automatically) by routing protocols (discussed in Chapter 6) or statically (manually). Routing tables will keep track of information such as the network address assigned to interfaces, subnet masks, route sources, destination network, and the outgoing interface etc.

Figure 2.4

Other key features of network routers include:
- The ability to filter on IP addresses;
- They don't forward broadcast or multicast packets;
- They perform packet switching;
- They perform packet filtering;
- They have path selection abilities to choose the best path of the next hop towards the destination address.

So, the bottom line is that if you have different networks (such as 192.168.1.0 and 192.168.2.0) and want to send data between the two, then you will need a router to do so, or at least a layer 3 switch that can perform routing functions.

Your home wireless router is actually doing the same thing as your network router in the office (to a degree) by routing traffic from your home network to the Internet, which, of course, is a network itself.

Firewall

When people think of a firewall they think of it as something to keep the bad guys out of their computer. While this is certainly true, firewalls can do much more than just offer protection from the outside world.

Firewalls can be a hardware based device (like in figure 2.5), or they can also run as software on a computer on your network. If you are a Microsoft Windows user, you might have noticed that you have the Windows Firewall installed on your computer, and it is usually preconfigured to where you don't have to do much with it. These locally installed firewalls are called host firewalls, and differ from a network firewall because they just protect the specific host that they are installed on.

Figure 2.5

As for hardware (or network) firewalls, they come in different varieties from the basic home unit to the expensive types (like shown in figure 2.5). These enterprise level firewalls are designed to perform various functions including:

- Monitoring of inbound and outbound traffic;
- Allowing or denying traffic based on preconfigured rules;
- Providing protection against threats;
- Allowing or denying traffic from other connected subnets;
- Providing VPN (virtual private network) access for remote users;

- Controlling user access to services such as web and FTP;
- Performing web content filtering.

You would place your hardware firewall between your internal network and the Internet to protect your network from outside threats and to filter traffic and services so that you can control what comes in and out of your network and what your end users can see and do. Figure 2.6 shows you the basic concept of how a firewall sits between the Internet and your internal network and controls access to data and services.

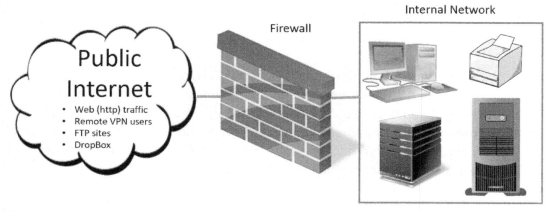

Figure 2.6

Now that you have an overview of the main hardware used with networking, let's put it all together in one diagram (figure 2.7). The configuration can vary depending on your needs. For example, you can have a router between the Internet and the firewall, and we can assume that the switches are layer 3 switches since they are "routing" traffic between two different networks.

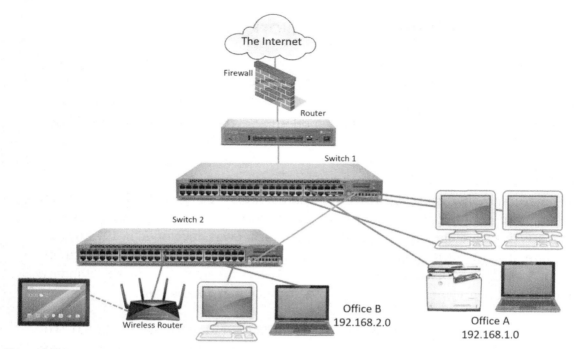

Figure 2.7

Chapter 3 – Network Cabling

In order to connect our devices to our network, we need some type of media in between them to allow for packets to get from one device to another. This is where network cabling comes into play. There are different types of cables you can use to connect your network, but with today's modern hardware there are only really two types that we tend to use.

Ethernet Cables

The most commonly used cables in today's datacenters are Ethernet cables. Ethernet is a standard of network communication using twisted pair cable, although coaxial cable was used in older versions of Ethernet. Ethernet was developed in 1973 by Bob Metcalfe at Xerox. It is the most widely used standard in network communication and runs at 10 to 1000Mbps (or 1Gbps), with 1Gbps speed now being the standard speed almost everywhere and 10Gbps and up gaining in popularity.

The most common Ethernet cabling in use today is Category 5e (or Cat5e) UTP (Unshielded Twisted Pair). This cable type utilizes four pairs of twisted-pair wires within one cable. Two pairs are used to send data, and two pairs are used to receive data. There is also a Shielded Twisted Pair (STP), but it is more expensive and harder to work with because of the shielding. Cat5 cables use an RJ-45 connector on the end, which looks like a phone cord connector only larger. Cat5e is a type of Cat5 cabling that supports 1Gbps connections where standard Cat5 only supports 100Mbps. Cat6 is the same as Cat5e except that it is made to a higher standard and increases the bandwidth from 100MHz to 250MHz. Cat7 is becoming more common as well.

Figure 3.1 shows a typical Ethernet cable along with a blown up image of the RJ45 connector that these cables use. There are eight wires within the cable, and the RJ45 connector has connection points for these eight wires.

Figure 3.1

The order of the wires inside the connector is critical in order for the cable to work properly. So is the actual connection of the wires within the connector, because if one of the wires is not making a connection, you will end up with a faulty cable. Straight through Ethernet cables are used to connect devices like computers and printers to switches, and the wire placement is the same on both ends of the cable. To connect devices such as a switch to another switch you would use a crossover cable (discussed next).

Even though RJ45 Ethernet cable connectors look like phone cable connectors (which are RJ11 connectors), it doesn't mean you should interchange them, even though you might be able to get a RJ11 cable to make a connection in a RJ45 port.

There are two standard wiring schemes for straight through Ethernet cables. They are either T568A or T568B, with T568B being the more commonly used wiring scheme in the US. The only difference between the two are that the pin positions for the green and orange pairs have been switched. Either one will work just fine on your network, but do not combine the two unless you want to have communication issues. Whether or not all four pairs are used is determined by the category of the cable. For example, an older 10/100Mbps cable would only use two pairs, while a 1Gbps cable would use all four pairs so it can transmit and receive at the same time.

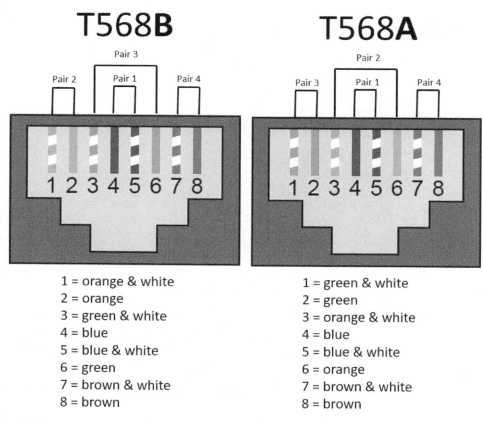

Figure 3.2

Some people like to make their own cables so they can determine their exact length. This is kind of a tedious process unless you get really good at it, plus you will need to test each cable you make with a cable tester to be sure it works properly.

Crossover Cables
Crossover cables are used to connect similar devices together such as a switch to switch, router to router, or a router connected directly to a host. These cables look and feel the same, but the wiring scheme is what makes them different. They are called crossover cables because one side is wired the opposite of the other side for four of the eight wires.

If you have been paying attention, you might have noticed that a crossover cable is basically a cable with the T568A wiring scheme on one side and the T568B wiring scheme on the other side.

To make things easy to remember, here is a chart listing what scenarios you would use a straight through cable for compared to a crossover cable.

Straight Through Cable	Crossover Cable
Computer to Switch Switch to Router Computer to Hub	Switch to Switch Router to Router Switch to Hub Hub to Hub Computer to Router Computer to Computer

Rollover Cables
One last type of cable I am going to mention is called a rollover cable, which is also referred to as a null modem cable (figure 3.3). These cables are used to connect a PC to a console port on a switch or router to perform management functions when you can't connect via one of the usual network ports.

The pin-outs on one end of a rollover cable are reversed at the opposite end. There is an RJ45 connection on one end and a DB9 connection on the other end. The RJ45 connection plugs into the switch or router's management port, and the DB9 will connect to a serial port on a computer. Most new computers don't have serial ports anymore, so you will need to use a USB to serial adapter in addition to the rollover cable. Some higher end switches now have micro USB ports for management so you can actually connect with a USB cable and even use your smartphone!

Rollover Cable
RJ45 on one end
DB9 connection on the other

Figure 3.3

Ethernet Cable Categories
Now that you know what an Ethernet cable is and how it's wired, I want to spend a little time discussing Ethernet cable categories. You might remember how I referred to a Cat5e cable earlier in the chapter, but that is not the only type of cable you can use. There were a few variations before Cat5e and a couple since then, and here is a quick summary of the Ethernet cable standards and their maximum speed capacity.

- **Category 3** – 10Mbps and 16Mhz frequency
- **Category 4** – 16Mbps and 20Mhz frequency
- **Category 5** – 100Mbps and 100Mhz frequency
- **Category 5e** – 1Gbps and 100Mhz frequency
- **Category 6** – 1Gbps and 250Mhz frequency
- **Category 6a** – 10Gbps and 500Mhz frequency
- **Category 7** – 100Gbps and 600Mhz frequency

These higher speeds (such as 1Gbps and above) are achieved by using four pairs of wires rather than just two, as well as increasing the twists per centimeter in the wire. Cat6 and above also has a nylon spline which helps to eliminate crosstalk, which is interference in one circuit that comes from another circuit. There is also another type of Ethernet cable called a shielded twisted pair (STP) that has a protective shielding wrapped around the wires to further prevent interference issues. STP cables are more expensive and harder to work with because they are not as flexible thanks to the shielding. When a cable doesn't have the shielding, it is known as an unshielded twisted pair or UTP cable.

99% of the time the type of Ethernet cable that you are working with will be printed on the jacket of the cable itself. You might just have to look at a couple of feet before you find it.

In general, Ethernet cables have a length limit of 100 meters (around 300 feet) before the signal starts to deteriorate and needs to be regenerated to carry on. Devices like hubs and switches will regenerate the signal so you can go another 100 meters before having to do it again.

Fiber Optic Cables

If you want to go fast and far at the same time, then you need to think about implementing fiber optic cables in your network. Let's begin our discussion by describing what a fiber optic cable is and how it works. Then I will go over the most common types in use today and compare it to the most current type of network cable (which is Ethernet cabling).

Fiber optic cables use glass or plastic tubes in the center of the cable to transmit data via a beam of light from a laser rather than copper wires used in other types of cabling (such as Ethernet). This part of the cable is referred to as the core. There is a glass cladding around the core that prevents light from escaping the inner core, then there is a plastic buffer around the cladding, and finally an outer jacket around the buffer (figure 3.4).

Because fiber optic cables use light rather than an electrical signal, they are not affected by RFI (radio frequency interference) or EMI (electro-magnetic interference). Using this method also allows for the use of longer cable runs because the signal does not have to be repeated or regenerated to keep its signal strength. Fiber optic cable does have distance limitations though, which varies depending on the type and speed. For example, 100Mbps cabling has a limit of 2 kilometers, which is 1.2 miles (or 6,561 feet), while 10Gbps cabling has a limit of only 300 meters (or around 1000 feet) depending on the specifications of the cable. Fiber optic cabling also comes in a 10Gbps speed with 40Gbps and 100Gbps starting to make their way into datacenters as well.

One important thing to keep in mind when comparing fiber optic cables to Ethernet cables is how you handle them. Making a fiber optic cable is a delicate process, and you can't just twist and bend them as you please when running them through your ceiling or wall because once you break the glass core, you are looking at replacing the cable. Ethernet cables have a little more give in how you can handle them since they use copper wires, which can take more abuse.

Single Mode vs. Multimode Cabling
There are two main fiber optic cable types in use today, and they are single mode and multimode. They differ in how they are made as well as the speed they can transmit data at and the distance it can send that data. Here are the key differences between the two:

Single Mode

- Smaller 9 micron core and a 125 micron cladding (prevents light from escaping).
- Only allows one mode of light to traverse through the cable, which lowers attenuation and allows the signal to travel further.
- Used for longer distance cable runs such as over a WAN.
- Higher bandwidth than multimode cabling.
- More expensive transceiver cost.
- Cheaper installation costs.

Multimode

- Larger 50 or 62.5 micron core and a 125 micron cladding.
- Allows multiple modes of light to traverse through the cable, allowing more data to pass through at a given time.
- Typically used within the datacenter with LANs.
- High bandwidth and speed over short to medium distances.
- Signal quality is reduced over long distances.
- Cheaper transceiver cost.
- More expensive installation costs.

Figure 3.4 shows a single mode and multimode cable cross section diagram.

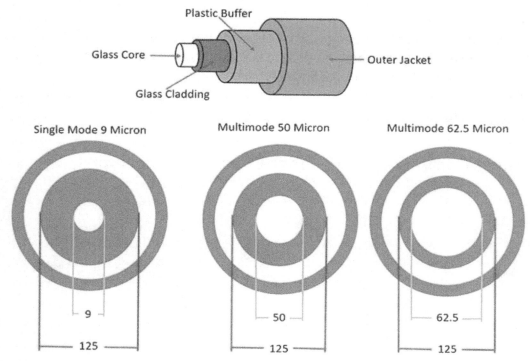

Figure 3.4

Figure 3.5 shows a single mode and multimode speed and distance chart so you can see how each type varies in performance. There are many versions of multimode cables labeled by OM, which refers to its optical multi-mode.

Cable Distance							
Cable Type		Fast Ethernet 100	1GB Ethernet - SX	1GB Ethernet - LX	10GB -SE-SR	40GB -SR4	100GB - SR10
Single Mode	OS2	200m	5000m	5000m	10km	X	X
Multimode	OM1	200m	275m	550m	X	X	X
Multimode	OM2	200m	550m	550m	X	X	X
Multimode	OM3	200m	550m	550m	300m	100m	100m
Multimode	OM4	200m	550m	550m	400m	150m	150m
Multimode	OM5	200m	550m	550m	300m	400m	400m

Figure 3.5

As for the cable connectors there are three main types that are in use today (figure 3.6). Sure there are others, but these three are the most common.

- **ST** - Stands for Straight Tip, and uses a keyed bayonet design is similar to that of a BNC connector and used mainly for MMF and SMF FOC. It uses a 2.5 mm ferrule.
- **LC** - Stands for Lucent Connector, and comes in three types (single mode LC APC, single mode LC UPC, and multimode LC UPC). It comes with a locking tab to keep it secure. It also uses a 2.5 mm ferrule.
- **SC** - Stands for Standard Connector, and is a low cost cable that also comes with a locking tab to keep it secure. It also uses a 2.5 mm ferrule.

Most Commonly Used Fiber Channel Cable Types

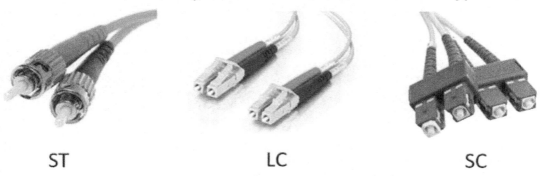

ST   LC   SC

Figure 3.6

As you can see, fiber channel is a fast and reliable cable medium, but there are a lot of factors you need to take into account before deciding if it's right for your network. With today's increased Ethernet speeds being applied to copper cables such as Category 6 and 7 cables, you have more options when it comes to deciding if you want to go the fiber optic route, or stick with copper. You also have to consider your budget since fiber optic cabling will be more expensive to install and maintain, especially if your IT staff is not familiar with how to take care of it and replace things when they fail. Plus, you need to make sure your network devices (such as your switches) can accept fiber optic connections and have the right type to match the cable type you want to use.

Simplex, Half Duplex, and Full Duplex Modes
Since we have been talking cable performance for some time now, let's go over signal speed or mode of operation really "quickly". There are three levels that are used to describe how a network connection operates, and they are simplex, half duplex, and full duplex.

- **Simplex** – Network communication only happens in one direction, which is not really too common because how often do we only communicate in one direction? But for cases where there are two or more communication channels, you can have each channel send the opposite direction of the other.
- **Half Duplex** – This is when communications are capable of going both directions, but can only happen one direction at a time. Think of it like when you use a Walkie-talkie and only one person can talk at a time.

- **Full Duplex** – In this mode, network communication can take place in both directions at the same time. You can think of this like a phone call, when both parties can talk and listen simultaneously.

In modern networks you will be using full duplex since it's important to be able to send and receive at the same time for the sake of network performance and to minimize collisions.

Cable Topologies
There are many ways to cable your network, and you need to choose what's best for you based on your hardware, ease of management, as well as your performance expectations. In today's modern networks we only really use one of them, which I will get to, but I wanted to go over some of the other topologies first so you can see what your options are and what we used to use in the past.

Bus
In a bus topology, every computer (or other device) is connected to a single network cable that it, therefore, connected to every other computer on the network (figure 3.7). The problem with this design is that if there is a break in the cable, all network communication is lost. One advantage is the simplicity and cost. This method works well in a small network, like something you would use at home, but if you use it in a large network, you are asking for performance issues and difficulty diagnosing problems.

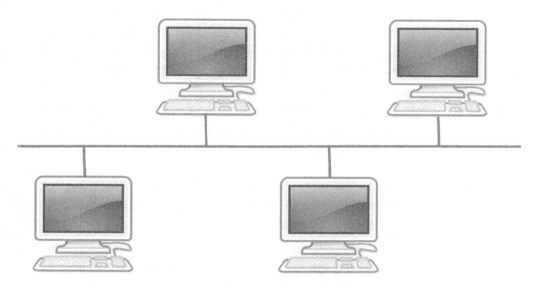

Figure 3.7

Ring

In a ring topology, all devices are connected to each other and the last device is connected to the first device to make a ring. Advantages to a ring topology is that you don't need any centralized switch and data collisions are minimized because the data flows in one direction around the ring. Data flow between devices can be fast, but since the data has to go to each device, network performance can be slow. On the other hand, if one computer shuts down, then the entire network will be affected since it will break the communication chain, and if you have a break in the cable, you will have the same type of problem.

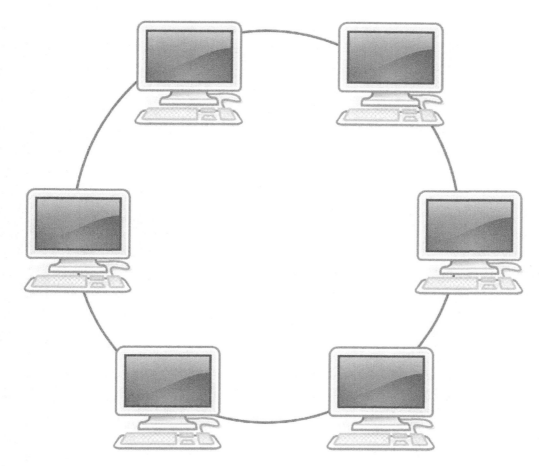

Figure 3.8

Mesh

In a mesh topology, each computer is connected to every other computer (figure 3.9). This provides redundancy because if a cable goes bad there are other paths that can be used by the computer to communicate with the other computers. This type of network can handle large amounts of traffic, since multiple devices can transmit data at the same time. On the downside, there is a higher cost associated with building a mesh topology, which also makes it harder to maintain.

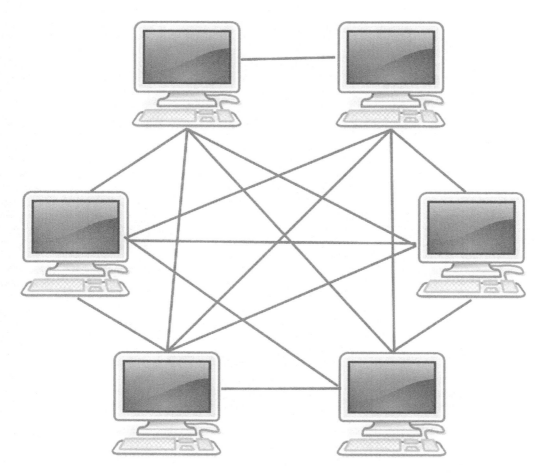

Figure 3.9

Star

The star topology is the most commonly used of the 4 topologies. It consists of a centralized device (most commonly being a switch) that all the computers connect to enable communications between each other. The star topology has several advantages, such as having a centralized point where computers and other network devices are connected, making management easier. If you need to add another device, you simply connect it to the switch and you are good to go (assuming it's configured correctly). If a computer or port on the switch fails, you don't have to worry about it affecting the other computers. One main disadvantage of a star topology is that if the centralized switch fails, then none of the computers will be able to communicate with each other. This is where having a backup switch comes in handy.

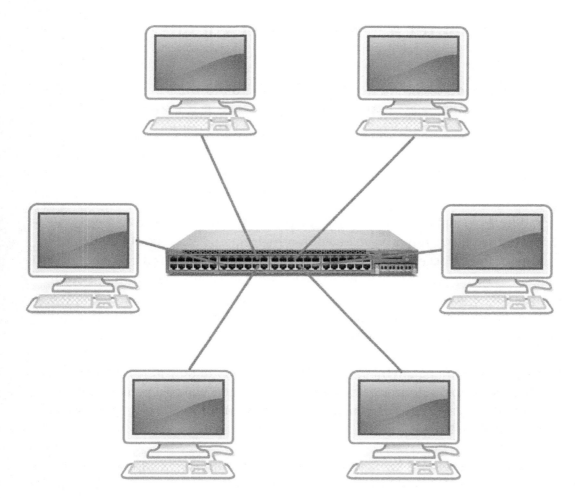

Figure 3.10

Chapter 4 – Wireless Networking

With the rapid growth of Internet connected device comes the increased usage of wireless (Wi-Fi) technologies. It seems as though everything is connected to the Internet these days, from our TVs to our refrigerators. With this increase in wireless usage comes an increase in wireless management to keep everything working properly.

Wireless Hardware

Wi-Fi (or Wireless Fidelity) works by transmitting data via radio waves from one device to another using radio waves at different frequencies. One of the devices needs to be a wireless access point or wireless router that has a wired connection to the main network. For home users, this main network is usually the Internet, but for users at the office you can have a wireless access point that connects you to the corporate network. This way you can do your normal work from places that might not have an Ethernet port to plug into for network access.

These access points can be anything from an inexpensive home wireless router to a full on industrial Cisco outdoor access point. A home router will cost you around $50 and up depending what features you want, where a corporate wireless router can run upwards of $1,500.

The device on the other end (usually a computer) needs to have a wireless adapter capable of receiving the Wi-Fi radio signals and then passing the data on to the device. Laptop computers have wireless adapters built-in, and most desktop computers are shipping with wireless adapters built-in as well. If you don't have one in your desktop and want to connect to your wireless Internet connection, then you can go out and get a USB Wi-Fi adapter and get yourself connected in about five minutes. As you can see in figure 4.1, there are a variety of wireless adapters to choose from.

Figure 4.1

Your smartphone will also have a wireless adapter built-in so you can connect to your home or office Wi-Fi and not have to use bandwidth from your expensive data plan. Plus, other devices like printers and even TVs have wireless adapters so they can be used on your network as well. As you can see from figure 4.2, you can connect many different types of devices to one wireless access point.

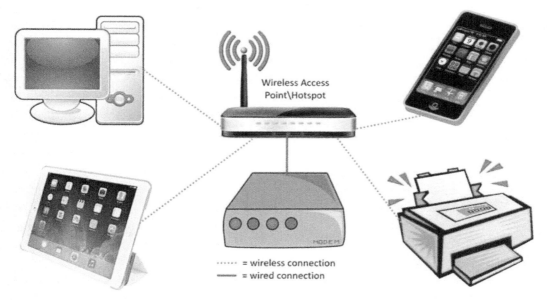

Figure 4.2

SSID

When you hear the term "wireless hotspot", that is just another name for a wireless access point, but it's usually referring to one in a public location like a coffee shop or restaurant. These hotspots use SSIDs, which are user-friendly connection names to advertise their location or purpose so you know what you are connecting to. You should always be cautious when connecting to a public hotspot because you never know who is behind the connection and what their intentions are. It's easy to fake a wireless name\SSID and trick you into connecting to that hotspot, making you vulnerable to their attacks.

You can easily change the SSID of your wireless connection at home or at the office by going into the settings of your access point/router and finding the appropriate section (figure 4.3). Normally you will access these settings via a web page that you connect to using the IP address of the access point itself. The IP address is usually the same one your computer uses for its default gateway. The manual should tell you what the default IP address is as well as the default username and password. Once you are in the settings, consider changing the username and password or at least the password because anyone who knows the defaults for your brand of access point has it that much easier to get into your network.

Wireless 2.4 GHz

Enable Wireless	☑ ?
Wireless Network Name (SSID)	Office ?
Pre-Shared Key	783R3ssrt! ?

More Wireless Settings...

Wireless 5 GHz

Enable Wireless	☑ ?
Wireless Network Name (SSID)	Office ?
Pre-Shared Key	783R3ssrt! ?

Figure 4.3

If you do change the default name and password for your access point, make sure to write it down somewhere secure because if you ever need to get into the settings again to change your Wi-Fi password etc. and can't get in, then you will be stuck resetting your access point back to the default and will lose any configuration and wireless passwords you have created.

If you lease your modem from your ISP and it has wireless capabilities built in, then it will usually have a sticker on the side of it with the SSID and password listed.

Wireless Standards

Now I would like to talk about wireless standards and how they have changed throughout the years. Wireless standards were put in place by the Electrical and Electronic Engineers (IEEE) to ensure wireless device manufacturers were all on the same page and that their devices would be compatible with each other. Over the years these standards improved features such as range and speed. These are just the main ones, and there are many other ones in between that were never really put into place.

Back in 1997, the 802.11 wireless standard was put into place. But it only supported a maximum network bandwidth of 2 Mbps (megabits per second), and therefore didn't last very long.

The replacement for 802.11 was called 802.11b. This came out in 1999, and offered bandwidth up to 11 Mbps. 802.11b uses a 2.4 GHz (gigahertz) frequency, which doesn't cost much to produce, but one of the downsides is that other electronic devices such as cordless phones and microwaves that use the same frequency can interrupt the wireless signal.

Along with 802.11b was 802.11a, but it wasn't widely accepted because of the cost. It was adapted more in business situations where they needed the faster speed and could afford the higher cost. It has a speed of 54 Mbps and uses a 5 GHz frequency, which helps reduce interference from other wireless devices.

Next came 802.11g, which came out in 2002. It also offers 54Mbps speed, but uses the 2.4 GHz frequency to obtain a greater range. They were also able to tweak things a little to help out with the interference problem with the 2.4 GHz frequency. Then, in 2009, came 802.11n, which used multiple antennas and signals to increase bandwidth and range. This technology is also called MIMO (multiple input, multiple output). 802.11n has a much higher speed at 300Mbps and better range than the older standards. It is also backward compatible with 802.11b and 802.11g devices, and can operate at 2.4 GHz and 5 GHz.

Then came 802.11ac in 2013, which had speeds of 450 Mbps on the 2.4 GHz frequency and 1300 Mbps on the 5 GHz frequency. It also has Multi-user MIMO (MU-MIMO) technology and is backwards compatible with the b, a, and g standards as well.

Eventually there will be newer standards that have even better range and speed.

Ad Hoc Mode and Infrastructure Mode
There are a couple of different ways you can connect your wireless devices, and each has their advantages. These modes are called Ad hoc and Infrastructure (figure 4.4).

Ad hoc mode (also known as peer to peer) allows each wireless device to communicate with each other without needing a hotspot or access point. This is great if you don't want to rely on a centralized access point, but one downside is that these devices can only communicate with other devices and not an access point. Security is not as robust as with using an access point because there is no central point of access. Setup can be easier since there is no access point involved, so if you have two devices that support ad hoc mode, they can communicate directly with each other. But, on the downside, each device has to establish a connection with every other device it intends to communicate with rather than just the access point.

Infrastructure mode is where each wireless device connects to an access point and then all the devices on the network communicate with each other via this access point. This mode is usually faster than Ad hoc mode, and security is increased as well. Plus, using infrastructure mode allows you to connect the access point to a wired network so wireless devices can access resources on that network. Infrastructure mode is better for a network that will stay in place and be up for an extended period of time, but if the central point of communication (access point) goes down, then nobody is talking with anybody. Infrastructure mode is more commonly used today.

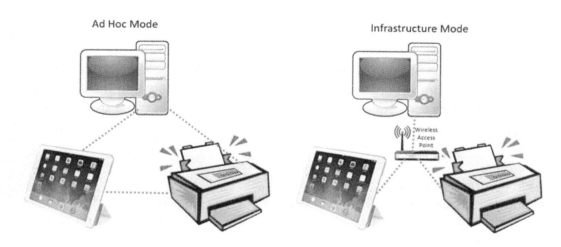

Figure 4.4

Security

Wi-Fi access points have security measures built-in to prevent anyone from connecting to anyone else's wireless network. They type of security measure you will use will depend on what the devices you want to connect to your wireless network support. You should always use the highest level that everything on your network supports.

There are three wireless security protocols I want to discuss, and they are WEP, WPA, and WPA2 (with WPA3 in the works). No matter what security protocol you use, it will never be as secure as a wired connection, because wireless signals are broadcast in the air for anyone to try and connect to. I will now go over the differences between these security protocols.

WEP (Wired Equivalent Privacy)

WEP was developed back in 1999, and then abandoned in 2004. It was specified in the IEEE Wireless Fidelity standard 802.11b and was intended to provide a wireless local area network (WLAN) with a level of security and privacy comparable to that of a wired LAN. It had a mechanism for encrypting data using user and system generated key values and offering password protection. These encryption keys started out at 64 bit, then were increased to 128 bit, and finally to 256 bit. WEP was commonly used with 802.11b/g routers. Eventually, researchers found out that WEP was far too easy to crack by hackers, so it was abandoned in favor of WPA.

WPA (Wi-Fi Protected Access)

In 2004, WPA was released to replace WEP and its flawed security features. WPA provides stronger encryption that WEP by using Temporal Key Integrity Protocol (TKIP) and Advanced Encryption Standard (AES). When a device connects to a WPA equipped router, keys are generated via a four way handshake between the device and the router, and then the connection is made. You might have also heard of WPA-PSK, and this is a form of WPA that uses a pre-shared key that is changed at intervals, making it harder to hack into the router.

WPA2 (Wi-Fi Protected Access 2)

WPA2 is an upgrade version of WPA, and is based on the IEEE 802.11i technology standard for data encryption. WPA2 offers stronger encryption than WPA and also uses pre-shared keys. It also makes use of Advanced Encryption Standard (AES) and CCMP, a TKIP replacement.

As for WPA3, it will offer improvements in authentication and encryption, will feature 192-bit encryption, and also make it harder for hackers to crack your password. Even if they do, it will limit what they are able to see once they get in. Normally hackers can attach to your wireless stream and then send it to their computer, which will run software designed to try and break your password. The good thing is if they get your password, they will only be able to decrypt new information they have obtained after getting the password but won't be able to decrypt any old information they might have got their hands on before getting your password.

Of course, with this new standard will come new hardware, so you will be buying a new wireless router if you want to use WPA3, and if your Wi-Fi functionality is provided by your broadband company's equipment, then they will be the ones needing to do the upgrade. Also keep in mind that your computer will need to support WPA3, but that will most likely be addressed with a software update.

Chapter 5 – IP Addressing

If you plan on getting into the networking field or even the IT field itself, you will need to learn about IP addresses and how they work, because a computer can't communicate on a TCP\IP network without one.

What is an IP Address?
There is an old yet still widely used analogy comparing IP addresses to street addresses that comes in handy when you're first getting into the concept of network addressing where you compare computer IP addresses to house street addresses and packets to packages or mail. If the postal carrier has a package that needs to be delivered to your house, they will need to know your address in order to get it there. And, of course, your address is unique to your street, so you can think of your house as your computer and your street as the network segment, with your computer having a unique address of its own on the network.

Right now we are mostly using IPv4 IP addresses for public (external) and private (internal) addressing. IPv4 addresses are 32 bit binary numbers that have four octets which can contain values from 0-255. An example of a common, privately used address is 192.168.1.20. You might see something like this assigned to your home computer from your broadband modem or wireless router. These types of IP addresses can be reasonably easy to remember depending on how many you have. If your network devices are on the same network or subnet, then each device will have a similar address, such as 192.168.1.30 and 192.168.1.32, so you only need to memorize the last number (octet) for each device. Then again, there is subnetting and address classes (discussed later) where it's not that simple, and you may have a more complicated address scheme going on, especially in larger networks with multiple subnets in multiple locations.

Subnet Masks
IP addresses have another component to them that determines what part of the IP address belongs to the network and what part identifies the host. This address (called a subnet mask) is also 32 bits like an IP address and is represented in four octets separated by periods. An example of a common subnet mask would be 255.255.255.0. There are default subnet masks for the A, B, and C classes of networks, which and I will be discussing classes later in this chapter. But, for now, here are the defaults for each class.

- Class A = 255.0.0.0
- Class B = 255.255.0.0
- Class C = 255.255.255.0

The way you determine what part of the subnet mask is for the network and what part is for the hosts is by converting the address to its binary number and using the 1s for network addresses and 0's for host addresses. So in our 255.255.255.0 example it would translate into 11111111.11111111.11111111.00000000, with all of the addresses in the first three octets belonging to the network and all of the last octet belonging to the hosts. (Binary numbering will be covered in a bit, so hopefully that will help this all make a little more sense if you are new to the concept.)

For most home users, and even home or small office configurations, a class C IP address and default subnet mask will work just fine because it allows you 254 network devices, which is most likely more than enough.

Default Gateway

One very important part of your computer's IP configuration is the default gateway. This is the IP address that is used when traffic from your network needs to leave the local network and get to a different network. The default gateway is usually the interface of your router or other layer 3 device that is used to pass traffic in and out of your local network. And by local network I mean the network that your computer is a part of. You may have just one network, or you can have many networks that are all connected together by routers or layer 3 switches.

As you can see in figure 5.1, when Computer 1 wants to communicate with Computer 4, it has to use its default gateway of 192.168.1.1 to get out of its local network (Network 1) and get to Computer 4, which is located in Network 2. Then the router will use its routing table or a routing protocol (discussed in Chapter 6) to determine where Computer 4 is located and pass the traffic along to its destination.

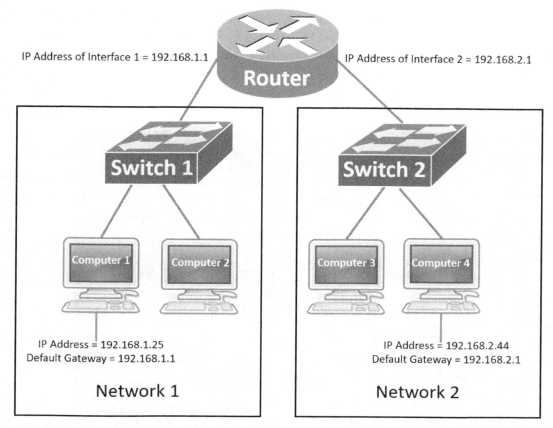

IP Address of Interface 1 = 192.168.1.1

IP Address of Interface 2 = 192.168.2.1

Router

Switch 1

Switch 2

Computer 1

Computer 2

Computer 3

Computer 4

IP Address = 192.168.1.25
Default Gateway = 192.168.1.1

IP Address = 192.168.2.44
Default Gateway = 192.168.2.1

Network 1

Network 2

Figure 5.1

You can assign a default gateway manually, or your DHCP server can do it for you. DHCP is usually a better option in large networks to avoid a lot of manual labor and potential mistakes. (DHCP is discussed later in this chapter.)

Finding Your IP Address
It's generally pretty easy to find the IP address of your computer or other device, and the method will vary depending on what device you are trying to find it on. Since Microsoft Windows is a very popular operating system, I will show you how to find your IP address on a Windows computer.

One very common way to find your IP address is from a command prompt. Command prompts are used to type in command line requests to the operating system in order to perform tasks or obtain information. It's similar to the old days of typing DOS commands. To open a command prompt, simply click on Start and type in **cmd** in the run or search box and press enter, or click on the Command Prompt or cmd.exe icon from the search results.

If you just want to find the basic IP address information you can type in **ipconfig** and press enter. You will get a listing similar to figure 4.2. If you have more than one network (Ethernet) adapter or a wireless connection, then you will get the same type of information for all of your connections.

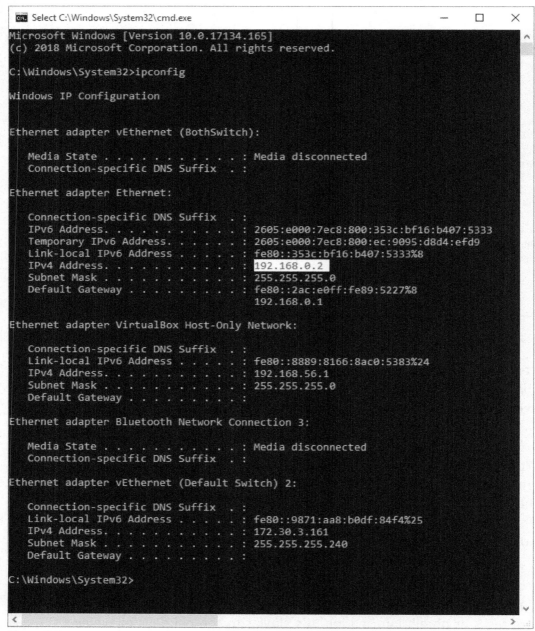

Figure 5.2

As you can see in my example, my IP address is 192.168.0.2 and my subnet mask is 255.255.255.0. If you want to get more detailed information, including your default gateway address, computer's host name, DHCP server address, etc., then use the same command but add the /all switch to the end so it looks like **ipconfig /all.** As you can see from figure 5.3, you get much more detailed information with the command.

Figure 5.3

You can also find your IP address using the GUI (graphical user interface), but the command prompt method is much faster. For other operating systems you can use their associated commands. For example, Linux and Apple computers use the ifconfig command rather than ipconfig command.

If you want to see what public IP address you are using for your Internet connection then do a Google search for "what is my ip" and try out one of the results from the search.

Manually Configuring an IP Address

IP addresses can be assigned statically (manually) or dynamically (automatically) by a DHCP server, but if you are the type that likes to do things yourself, then it's easy to assign an IP address to your computer manually. Before doing so you just need to make sure you have all the appropriate information handy, otherwise you could be looking at communication problems.

Once again I will stick to the Microsoft Windows method of manually assigning an IP address, and this time we will do it from the GUI. Keep in mind that this method may vary a little depending on what version of Windows you are running.

What you need to do is go into the Windows Control Panel and find Network and Sharing Center. Then click on the link on the left that says *Change adapter settings*. Then find the network adapter that you are currently using in the list. You might only have one, and if that's the case it makes things easier.

Next you should right click on the appropriate adapter and choose *Properties*, and from the Networking tab click on *Internet Protocol Version 4* and click *Properties* again.

If your computer is set to get its IP address automatically from a DHCP server, then your properties box will look similar to figure 5.4.

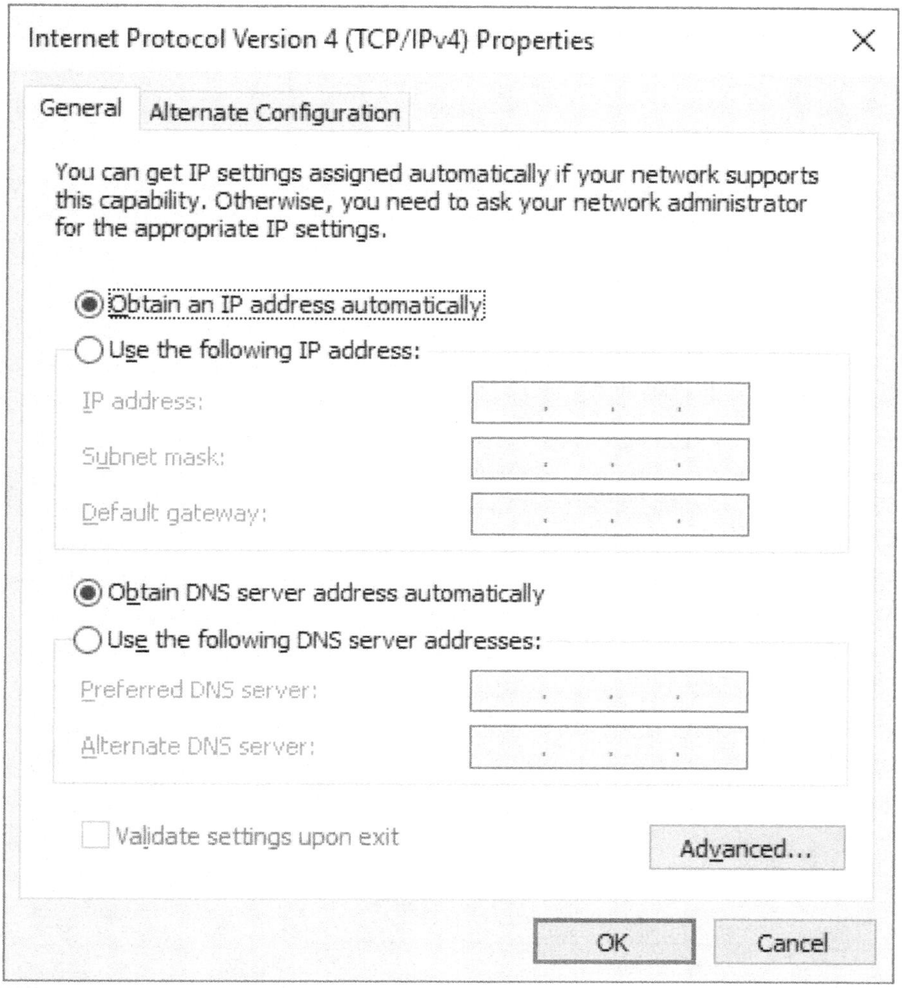

Figure 5.4

To manually assign an IP address to your computer click on the radio button that says *Use the following IP address* and enter in the appropriate information for the IP address, subnet mask, and default gateway (figure 5.5). Just make sure the IP address you use is not in use on your network by any other device. For the DNS settings you will need to find out what DNS servers are being used on your network (DNS is covered in Chapter 6).

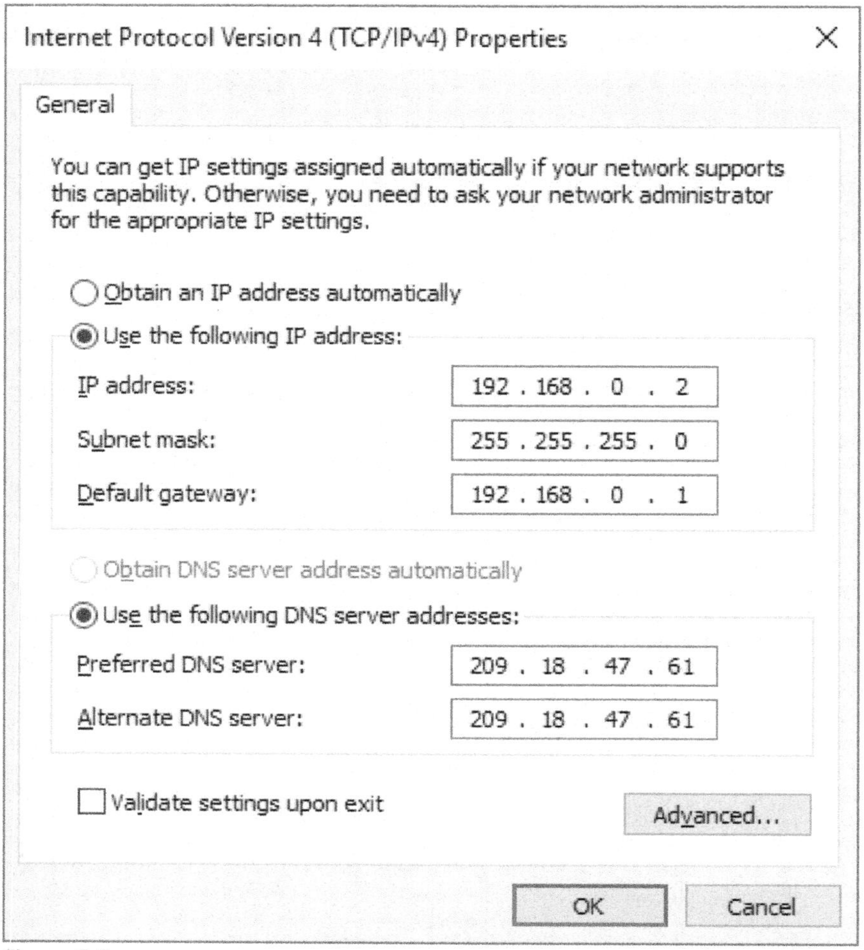

Internet Protocol Version 4 (TCP/IPv4) Properties   ✕

General

You can get IP settings assigned automatically if your network supports
this capability. Otherwise, you need to ask your network administrator
for the appropriate IP settings.

○ Obtain an IP address automatically

◉ Use the following IP address:

IP address:	192 . 168 . 0 . 2
Subnet mask:	255 . 255 . 255 . 0
Default gateway:	192 . 168 . 0 . 1

○ Obtain DNS server address automatically

◉ Use the following DNS server addresses:

Preferred DNS server:	209 . 18 . 47 . 61
Alternate DNS server:	209 . 18 . 47 . 61

☐ Validate settings upon exit   Advanced...

OK   Cancel

Figure 5.5

If your network is using DHCP for IP address distribution, then you can leave the DNS settings set to automatic while having the IP settings set to manual, and you will get the DNS settings configured automatically for you.

DHCP
Since I have mentioned DHCP a few times in this book I figure now is a good time to go into a little more detail about what it is and how it works because your network will most likely be using DHCP whether it's a large network or a small one.

DHCP stands for Dynamic Host Configuration Protocol, and it was designed to simplify the management of IP address configuration by automating this configuration for network clients. All computers that participate on TCP/IP networks or the Internet need to have IP addresses assigned to them and have other IP information configured.

Some of the additional information needed by network clients may include a subnet mask, default gateway, and DNS server information. This information is needed in order for the computer to do things such as send data outside the network and resolve host names to IP addresses. Rather than manually inputting all of this information on each client, DHCP can do this for you automatically once it's setup on the DHCP server.

In order for DHCP to work, you need to have a device acting as a DCHP server. This device can be a computer, router or other type of network device. The DHCP server is configured with a range or ranges of IP addresses that can be used to give to clients that request one. It can also be configured with other network parameters, as stated earlier.

For a client to be able to obtain information from a DHCP server, it must be DHCP enabled. When it is configured this way, then it will look for a DHCP server when it starts up. This process will vary depending on what implementation of DHCP is in use. For example, the Microsoft implementation of DHCP works as follows:

- The client sends out a DHCPDiscover packet the first time the client attempts to log on to the network.

- Then the DHCP server that receives the DHCPDiscover packet responds with a DHCPOffer packet which contains an un-leased IP address and any additional TCP/IP configuration information.

- When a DHCP client receives a DHCPOffer packet, it then responds by broadcasting a DHCPRequest packet that contains the offered IP address, and shows acceptance of the offered IP address.

- The selected DHCP server acknowledges the client DHCPRequest for the IP address by sending a DHCPAck packet and then the client can access the network.

- DHCP clients try to renew their lease when fifty percent of the lease time has expired by sending a DHCPRequest message to the DHCP server. They also send this message when they restart to try and get the same IP configuration back.

The amount of time a client keeps its lease on its IP address varies depending on how it is setup. The default Microsoft duration is eight days, and most computers end up with the same IP address they had before when it comes time to renew.

If the client computer is setup to use DHCP to obtain its IP address and cannot find a DHCP server, then it will most likely use an APIPA (Automatic Private IP Addressing) address instead. When using APIPA, DHCP clients can automatically self-configure an IP address and subnet mask for themselves when a DHCP server is not available. The IP address range used by APIPA is 169.254.0.1 through 169.254.255.254 with a class B subnet mask of 255.255.0.0. The client will use this self-configured IP address until a DHCP server becomes available. So, if you are trying to configure your new router at home and notice your IP address is 169.254.x.x when running the ipconfig command, then it's most likely because it can't get an IP address from the router.

With DHCP, you can also do things like reserve an IP address for a specific computer or exclude a range of IP addresses so they will not be given out to DHCP clients. Plus there are special settings called *options* where you configure things such as your DNS and gateway (router) configurations so they are given to clients along with the IP address settings.

Default IP Address Classes
As I mentioned earlier, there are two parts to an IP address you need to know about: the network portion and the host portion. This will determine how many addresses are reserved for different networks and how many are reserved for the hosts on those networks. There are designated classes (also called classful addressing) that help to keep the network and host addresses in order, and these are the main ones. Remember that octets are the numbers between the dots of the IP address, so it looks like octet1.octet2.octet3.octet4.

- **Class A**—The first octet is for the network address, and the last three octets are the host addresses. An IP address that has a number between 1 and 126 in the first octet is a Class A address.
- **Class B**—The first two octets are for the network address, and the last two octets are the host addresses. An IP address that has a number between 128 and 191 is a Class B address.
- **Class C**—The first three octets are for the network address, and the last octet is the host address. The first octet range of 192 to 223 is a Class C address.
- **Class D**—These are used for multicast addresses and have their first octets in the range of 224 to 239.
- **Class E**—Reserved for future use and has the range of addresses in the first octet from 240 to 255.

You might have noticed that the IP address starting with 127 is missing from the list. This is because its reserved for loopback functionality meaning that datagrams sent to a network 127 address should loop back inside the host. In other words the datagram will make a loop and return back to itself. This is used for testing purposes and 127.0.0.1 is the most commonly used loopback IP address.

When you use these default classes of IP addresses it's pretty straightforward, but when you get into subnetting where you are dividing one network into two or more networks to adjust the available number of networks or hosts you can use, then you start to get into what they call Classless Inter-Domain Routing, or CIDR. (Subnetting is discussed later in this chapter.)

With IPv4 there are about 4.3 billion total addresses, and the ones that are publicly owned cannot be used in more than one place. Private IP address can be used in multiple locations as long as they are not duplicated on the same internal network. We are officially out of public IPv4 IP addresses, so now we will need to start implementing IPv6 in order to continue. IPv6 is already being implemented, and though it has not been widely accepted yet, it will be soon enough.

Binary Numbering with IP Addresses
You may or may not have heard the term ones and zeros when people talk about computers and networking. What they are referring to is the binary numbering system which computers use to function with a 1 digit representing on and a 0 digit representing off. Each of these 1s or 0s we use represent a bit, and an IP address contains 32 bits.

Since the highest value of an octet for an IP address is 255, we only need to worry about knowing the binary values from 0-255. And the way we do this is by having a range of standard numbers that we are used to, and then convert them to binary based on whether we need to use that number or not. This range of numbers is as follows:

128   64   32   16   8   4   2   1

Now, in order to determine which numbers are being used and which are not, we would put a 1 for the value of a number we need to use and then a 0 for a number we don't need to use. For example, if we needed to figure out what the number 16 is in binary, we give the number 16 from the list above a value of 1 for on and the rest of the numbers a 0, so it would look something like this:

128	64	32	16	8	4	2	1
0	0	0	1	0	0	0	0

So 16 in binary = 00010000. That is a pretty simple example, so let's try something a little more complicated. What would 207 be in binary? Just because it's a larger number doesn't mean it has to be any harder. Simply calculate it the same way, but this time use the numbers that are required to come up with 207 and start from the left.

128	64	32	16	8	4	2	1
1	1	0	0	1	1	1	1

As you can see 128 + 64 + 8 + 4 + 2 + 1 = 207

Now if we apply the same math to an entire IP address, we will get its binary equivalent. Let's use one of the IP addresses that I have been using so far, which was 192.168.1.20, and convert it to binary.

192 = 11000000
168 = 10101000
1 = 00000001
20 = 00010100

Now we put it all together and come up with:
11000000.10101000.00000001.00010100

As you can see, the concept of binary numbers is not really difficult, but things start to get more interesting (and complicated) when you get into Classless Inter-Domain Routing (CIDR) and subnetting.

If you don't feel like doing the decimal to binary conversion in your head or on a piece of paper, then you can use the Windows calculator to do it for you. Just change the type of calculator in Windows to Programmer.

Classless Inter-Domain Routing (CIDR)

CIDR is an IP addressing scheme that allows us to customize the allocation of IP addresses. Think of it as a replacement for the original A, B, and C classful scheme that was mentioned earlier in this chapter. CIDR was designed to extend the life of IPv4 by allowing us a method to conserve IP addresses until we are ready for IPv6. Going back to our original class A, B, and C scheme, as you can see we are stuck with set numbers of network and hosts IDs per network class.

- Class A – 126 possible networks and 16,277,214 hosts.
- Class B – 16,384 possible networks and 65,535 hosts.
- Class C – 2,097,152 possible networks and 254 hosts.

Let's say you needed more than 300 hosts on a network. You wouldn't be able to use a class C address and would have to go with a class B address. But then you would be wasting thousands of hosts because you only needed 300 and now have 16,384.

These default address classes have their default subnet masks, and these masks can be written in the / (slash) format (also called CIDR notation), making it shorter than writing out the entire subnet mask.

- Class A mask – 255.0.0.0 or 11111111.00000000.00000000.00000000
- Class B mask – 255.255.0.0 or 11111111.11111111.00000000.0000000
- Class C mask – 255.255.255.0 or 11111111.11111111.11111111.00000000

Now if you count the number of 1's in the subnet mask, you will get your slash format number.

- Class A - 11111111.00000000.00000000.00000000 = /8
- Class B - 11111111.11111111.00000000.0000000 = /16
- Class C - 11111111.11111111.11111111.00000000 = /24

CIDR borrows bits from the host portion of the subnet mask to be used for the network mask which allows you to make adjustments as to how many possible networks and hosts you can have on a network. So if you take a class C subnet mask and borrow two of the host bits to increase your amount of network bits, it would look like this:

11111111.11111111.11111111.11000000 = /26

As you can see, now it's a /26 because we have 26 1s in the subnet mask. This is where subnetting comes into play, so let's start that discussion now.

Basic Subnetting

In order to solve the problem mentioned above about having a limited set of networks and hosts when using the classful IP addressing scheme, we now use subnetting to get the results we need to make our network design work for us. I am going to give a brief overview of subnetting because there is so much to it that you can write a book on it. It's beyond the scope of this book, otherwise it would be called Networking Made Difficult!

Before we begin, let's look at the class A, B, and C network (N) and host (H) defaults for subnet masks.

Class A network
N.H.H.H 255.0.0.0

Class B network
N.N.H.H 255.255.0.0

Class C network
N.N.N.H 255.255.255.0

To determine the number of networks and hosts that can be used with a particular subnet mask, you need to do a little math and use your binary skills. It's also a good idea to know your power of 2s when doing the calculations. (Or you can just use a subnet calculator and not worry about it!)

One thing you have to be aware of is what class of IP address you are subnetting because that will determine where you start counting the network bits to be used. Let's use a class A address, which uses the 4th octet for subnetting.

For our example we have a class C IP address with a subnet mask of 255.255.255.224. You might have noticed that the subnet mask is different than the standard class C 255.255.255.0 subnet mask. You might remember how 255.255.255.0 converts to binary.

255.255.255.0 = 11111111.11111111.11111111.0 or /24 because of the 24 1s.

In that case, our subnet mask of 255.255.255.224 converts as follows:

255.255.255.224 = 11111111.11111111.11111111.11100000 or /27 because of the 27 1s.

128	64	32	16	8	4	2	1
1	1	1	0	0	0	0	0

128 + 64 + 32 = 224

We have taken three bits from the host portion of the address, since we originally had 24 and now have 27 1s for our network portion of the subnet mask. To determine how many networks and how many hosts we can get from this subnet mask, we will start our calculations. To get the number of available networks you take the number of network bits (1s) used for the particular type of address (11100000). In our case it's 3, because we are using the last octet for subnetting purposes, and take that number to the power of 2. So we have $2^3 = 8$ networks.

Then we take the number of 0s to the power of 2 which in our case is $2^5 = 32$. But we can't use the first and last address in a network because .0 represents the network address itself and .255 is the broadcast address, so, in reality, to get the number of hosts per network we use $2^5 - 2 = 30$.

With the /27 subnet masks we end up with 8 different networks with 30 hosts allowed per network rather than the default class C subnet mask, giving us 2,097,152 possible networks with 254 hosts on each one, which more than any one person or company would ever use. This comes in handy for places like ISPs who have to give out public IP addresses, but don't want to waste any at the same time. You can use subnetting on your internal network to change the number of networks or hosts that you have available to fine tune your IP address scheme.

Here is a shortcut chart you can use to match the number of bits turned on for each subnet mask number. It's a good idea to know the numbers from 128 to 255 for each bit that is turned on.

.0 = 00000000
.128 = 10000000
.192 = 11000000
.224 = 11100000
.240 = 11110000
.248 = 11111000
.252 = 11111100
.254 = 11111110
.255 = 11111111

VLANs

As networks started getting larger, with more hosts being added to these networks, it became necessary to break these networks up to cut down on the amount of broadcast domains in a switched network. Segregating networks with routers internally is not practical, so this is where VLANs come into play. A virtual LAN is a logical grouping of network devices and resources connected to ports on a switch that have been designated for that virtual LAN. This allows you to have smaller broadcast domains when using layer 2 switches.

By using VLANs, you can create specific network segments or subnets for groups of users such as finance and keep their traffic together while separating them from other groups of users such as sales or marketing. To do this, let's say you have a 48 port switch and you assign the finance department a VLAN number of 200. On ports 1-12 you make them members of VLAN 200 and connect finance users to any of the ports from 1-12 so they will be able to communicate with each other. Then you can assign other ports to different VLANs for different purposes like in figure 4.6.

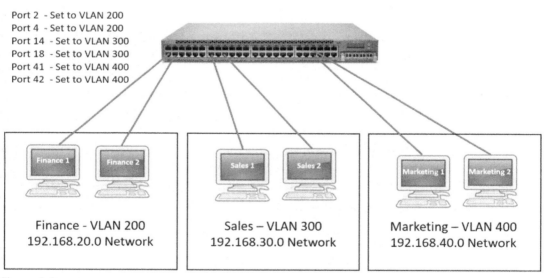

Figure 5.6

But what if you want some computers on one VLAN to be able to talk to computers on a different VLAN? This is where you will need to implement Inter-VLAN Routing or IVR. IVR is a way to route traffic from one VLAN to another, but to do this you will need to use switches that have layer 3 (routing) capabilities (unless you plan on having to use routers on your network, which will just add complexity and added cost).

Another hurdle to VLANs is the fact that you may need to get traffic from these VLANs to other parts of your network that are separated by switches. Sure you can route traffic from VLAN to VLAN on the same switch using IVR, but what about from one switch to another? To accomplish this we need to implement VLAN Trunking Ports. These ports will pass VLAN traffic from one switch to another through one port. The trunk port in figure 4.7 can carry traffic from VLAN 10, 20, 30, and 40.

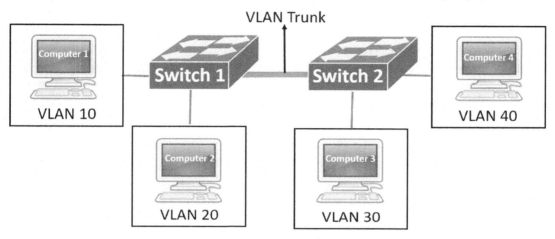

Figure 5.7

To implement this switch to switch VLAN communication, you will need to use the VLAN Trunking Protocol, or VTP.

IPv4 vs. IPv6
I have been talking about IP addresses quite a bit and have kept the discussion to version 4, but now it's time to look to the future and talk about version 6 (or IPv6, as it's known). Right now we are mostly using IPv4 IP addresses for public (external) and private (internal) addressing, and as you know, IPv4 addresses are 32 bit binary numbers that have four octets that can contain values from 0-255. Once again, an example of a commonly used private IP address is 192.168.1.20, and you might see something like this assigned to your home computer from your broadband modem or wireless router. These types of IP addresses can be reasonably easy to remember depending on how many you have, and if your network devices are on the same network or subnet, then each device will have a similar address (such as 192.168.1.30 and 192.168.1.43), so you only need to memorize the last number (octet) for each device in this example.

With IPv4 there are about 4.3 billion total addresses, and the ones that are publicly owned cannot be used in more than one place. Private IP address can be used in multiple locations as long as they are not duplicated on the same internal network.

We are officially out of public IPv4 IP addresses, so now we will need to start implementing IPv6 in order to continue. IPv6 is already being implemented, but has not been widely accepted yet. However, it will be soon enough.

IPv6 will allow us to have 340,282,366,920,938,463,463,374,607,431,768,211,456 IP addresses (or 2^{128} to make it easier to read). It also uses a 128 bit address space rather than a 32 bit address space like IPv4 uses. One problem with IPv6 is that it is not compatible with IPv4, making it more difficult to implement with today's primarily IPv4 address scheme. There are some methods that have been developed to make the communication work between the two to get around the problem.

IPv6 addresses are displayed as eight groups of four hexadecimal digits, with these groups being separated by colons (:). Here is an example of an IPv6 address (2605:e000:7ec8:0800:006f:10f6:1394:0370). As you can see, there are letters as well as numbers in the address. Hexadecimal numbers allow the use of the numbers 0-9 and the letters A-F (representing 10-15), and with this many IPv6 addresses, it's said that every device in the world will be able to have its own unique, publicly routed IP address. If you are on a Windows computer, you can run ipconfig /all and see that you have both an IPv4 and IPv6 IP address assigned to your network adapter (unless, of course, you have IPv6 disabled) (figure 5.8).

```
Wireless LAN adapter Wi-Fi:

   Connection-specific DNS Suffix  . :
   Description . . . . . . . . . . . : Intel(R) Dual Band Wireless-AC 3168
   Physical Address. . . . . . . . . : 30-E3-7A-35-EE-63
   DHCP Enabled. . . . . . . . . . . : Yes
   Autoconfiguration Enabled . . . . : Yes
   IPv6 Address. . . . . . . . . . . : 2605:e000:7ec8:800:647a:40ff:c255:736a(Preferred)
   Temporary IPv6 Address. . . . . . : 2605:e000:7ec8:800:596f:10f6:1394:5370(Preferred)
   Link-local IPv6 Address . . . . . : fe80::647a:40ff:c255:736a%11(Preferred)
   IPv4 Address. . . . . . . . . . . : 192.168.0.5(Preferred)
   Subnet Mask . . . . . . . . . . . : 255.255.255.0
   Lease Obtained. . . . . . . . . . : Saturday, December 23, 2017 1:11:50 PM
   Lease Expires . . . . . . . . . . : Saturday, December 23, 2017 3:48:36 PM
   Default Gateway . . . . . . . . . : fe80::2ac:e0ff:fe89:5227%11
                                       192.168.0.1
   DHCP Server . . . . . . . . . . . : 192.168.0.1
   DHCPv6 IAID . . . . . . . . . . . : 170976122
   DHCPv6 Client DUID. . . . . . . . : 00-01-00-01-21-70-72-DA-12-00-15-B7-46-92
   DNS Servers . . . . . . . . . . . : 209.18.47.61
                                       209.18.47.62
   NetBIOS over Tcpip. . . . . . . . : Enabled
```

Figure 5.8

There are ways to shorten how an IPv6 address is written, making it easier to wrap your head around the number and also to avoid getting something wrong when making a note of an address. One thing you can do is remove any leading 0's in the address to shorten it a bit. So, our example address of

2605:e000:7ec8:0800:006f:10f6:1394:0370

Can then be shortened to
2605:e000:7ec8:800:6f:10f6:1394:370.

Another thing you can do to shorten an IPv6 address is to replace any blocks that have consecutive 0's (0000:0000) with colons. So if we had an address like 2564:0000:0000:5fb7:05a2:1557:00b3:f9c4

We can shorten it even further to
2564::5fb7:5a2:1557:b3:f9c4.

There are three main types of IPv6 addresses, and they are Link-Local Address, Global Unicast Address, and Unique-Local Address. Here is the difference between them:

- **Link-Local Address** – This is an auto-configured IPv6 address that always starts with FE80, and are used on only broadcast segments and are never routed. They refer to a specific physical link and are used for addressing on a single link for things like automatic address configuration and neighbor discovery protocol.
- **Global Unicast Address** – These addresses are globally identifiable and uniquely addressable. They consist of a 64 bit subnet ID and a 64 bit interface ID.

- **Unique-Local Address** – These addresses are globally unique, but they should be used in local communication only and always start with FD. Use these for devices that will never communicate on the Internet.

IPv6 also has some other advantages\features that IPv4 doesn't, making it a worthy replacement after all the hard work is done. Some of these advantages include the following:

- Auto configuration for ease of implementation;
- No need to use NAT (Network Address Translation);
- Larger amount of multicast addresses;
- Increased throughput and efficiency with larger payloads;
- More efficient routing and smaller routing tables;
- Better security (encryption and IPsec built-in);
- Easier and cheaper to manage once implemented (better scalability);
- Improved mobility capabilities;
- No need for checksum verification;

- Devices can be connected to multiple networks at the same time;
- Faster speed because of less fragmentation;
- Quality of Service (QOS) built into packet header;
- IP addresses can be assigned automatically and dynamically by the client, eliminating the need for a DHCP server.

So, as you can see, there is quite a difference between IPv4 and IPv6, and there is much more to it in addition to what we have gone over here. Once the hard part of implementing IPv6 and replacing IPv4 IP addresses in the distant future is complete, we will all be better off (except for maybe the network administrators who have to become experts at it!).

MAC Addresses

Even though MAC address and an IP address are not the same thing, I want to mention MAC addresses here since they still apply to networking, and they are used in communications between computers when they are on the same subnet.

A MAC (Media Access Control) address is a unique identifier that is assigned to a network device by the manufacturer. It's a 48 bit hexadecimal number and looks like 12-00-15-B7-46-92. They are also known as a hardware addresses, burned in addresses (BIA), or physical addresses. Every network adapter, switch port, wireless card, etc. has its own unique MAC address.

MAC addresses are used at the Data Link Layer (layer 2) of the OSI Model, and are used for network communications between devices on the same subnet where no routing needs to be performed. As I mentioned before, switches use MAC filter tables (also known as Content Addressable Memory tables) to store information about known devices and their MAC addresses. Then when some type of network communication needs to happen, the switch can send the data directly to the device because it knows exactly which port on the switch that device is connected to. These table entries will expire eventually, and if the switch loses power then they will have to be repopulated over time once it's powered back on.

Most modern operating systems will let you change your MAC address or "spoof" it in case you need to alter it for a particular reason. For example, some software licenses are tied to the MAC address and if you get a new network card the MAC address will be different and you can give your computer back the old MAC address to make the software work again.

Chapter 6 – Protocols

There is a lot more to networking than just connecting the cables from your computers to your switches etc., but it would be nice if it were really that simple. Networks rely not only on hardware to get the job done, but also software that runs on the networking equipment as well as your computer or other device. In this chapter I am going to discuss various networking protocols that are used in today's networks to keep the data flowing.

Think of protocols as sets of rules and procedures that govern how communication is handled between network devices. They have mechanisms that identify and make connections, as well as determine how information is packaged for network transmission.

TCP\IP
TCP\IP, or Transmission Control Protocol\Internet Protocol, was designed by the Department of Defense (DoD) in 1973 as a safeguard to preserve data in case of a catastrophic war situation. It consists of a suite of communication protocols used to interconnect network devices on the internet and our internal networks. TCP\IP is the core of networking protocols, and without it we would still be sending faxes and memos to each other.

The DoD has its own model of the networking process, and it's similar to the OSI Model, but only has four layers compared to seven. The DoD Model has some layers that cover multiple layers of the OSI Model. The four layers of the DoD Model include:

- Process\Application Layer
- Transport Layer
- Internet Layer
- Link Layer

As you can see from figure 6.1, the DoD layers match up to the OSI layers, but two of the DoD layers match up to multiple OSI layers.

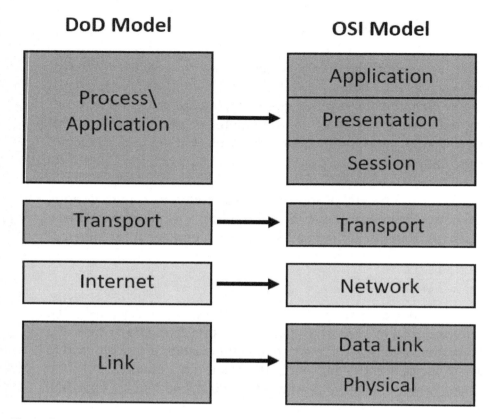

Figure 6.1

Within these layers you will find various protocols that have specific functions, and many of them you might recognize from your daily computer\network activities. Keep in mind that there are many protocols in use in today's networks, but I'm going to focus on the some of the more commonly used and important ones.

Application Layer Protocols

The application layer has a very large amount of network protocols contained in it, and they are some of the most commonly used protocols in use today. I will now go over many of them and tell you what they are used for.

- **HTTP** – HTTP (or Hypertext Transfer Protocol) is one of the most widely used protocols because it's the protocol used by the Internet and our web browsers to get our web pages sent to our computers and other devices. Your browser uses a URL such as **http**://www.onlinecomputertips.com to find the server for the website that you are looking for.

- **HTTPS** – The secure version of HTTP is called HTTPS, and it uses SSL (Secure Socket Layer) to make the connection between your computer and the web server secure. HTTPS connections will always be used for things like banking sites or other websites that require a login. When going to a site that you think should be secure, make sure it has the S in the URL, such as https://mybanksite.com.

- **DNS** – When you connect to a networked computer by name or type in a website URL in your browser, you are using the Domain Name Service to translate that name into its associated IP address. This process is called resolving a hostname. Keep in mind that you can also access networked devices and websites by their IP address, and sometimes you have to do this when DNS is not working or doesn't know how to resolve the name properly. There are public DNS servers on the Internet that resolve website addresses and also internal DNS servers in your network to resolve host names of network devices.

- **DHCP** – The Dynamic Host Configuration Protocol was discussed in detail in Chapter 4, but, to review, it's a service that assigns IP addresses to network enabled devices so they can communicate on the network.

- **Telnet** – Telnet was developed for terminal emulation of the device it is connected to. It's a client server type of situation where you connect to a device running a Telnet server with your Telnet client. Once you make this connection, Telnet acts as though you are using the actual remote machine. The main problem with Telnet is that everything is sent in clear text, so it's not secure. Many admins still use it for switch and router maintenance anyway.

- **SSH** – SSH stands for Secure Shell, and its similar to Telnet except that it offers secure connections using encryption. It can be used to connect to all kinds of devices and is the preferred way to manage your switches and routers because of its security features.

- **FTP** – The File Transfer Protocol has been around forever and provides the ability to transfer files between systems. One device needs to be running a FTP service and the other device typically uses an FTP client to connect to the FTP server. This can be done with a graphical program, or also from the command line. There is also a basic version of FTP called TFTP (Trivial File Transfer Protocol) that is commonly used to save and copy switch configurations.

- **SNMP** – The Simple Network Management Protocol is used to collect and analyze information from network devices and then report issues that are out of the norm to administrators as needed. It uses Network Management Stations (NMS) to poll devices that you set up to be monitored. Then agents send alerts called traps to the NMS when there is an issue.

- **NTP** – Computers on a network need to have their system times really close to each other to be able to function properly. The Network Time Protocol service does this by acting as a service to point the computers to a time server that they can synchronize themselves with so all the devices on the network have the same time. You can use an internal time server or have the devices get their time from a public time server on the Internet.

Transport Layer Protocols
After the Application Layer comes the Transport Layer, which performs such functions as message segmentation, traffic control, sending acknowledgements, performing session multiplexing, and performing error detection and correction. The two man protocols used at this layer are TCP and UDP.

- **TCP** – The Transmission Control Protocol is one of the most commonly used protocols in use today thanks to the Internet, and is part of the TCP/IP protocol suite. TCP ensures end to end delivery of data, and works in alongside with the Internet Protocol (or IP). It takes large blocks of data from applications and breaks them into segments and numbers and sequences them so they can be put back into the order that the application intended them to be in for the destination.

  TCP is what they call "connection oriented", meaning that there is a connection that is made before any data is sent. This makes it a reliable protocol because if there is any data that doesn't make it because of errors or congestion, then it will be resent, assuring there are no lost packets. TCP also does error checking and recovery to assure its reliability. Because of the factors that make it reliable, TCP has a lot of overhead to go along with it. With today's networks becoming more reliable, many technologies are using UDP instead to increase performance, but with this performance comes a cost.

- **UDP** – The User Datagram Protocol is a scaled down version of TCP that doesn't require as much overhead or bandwidth on the network as TCP does. UDP is a connectionless protocol, which means it doesn't offer the reliability and guaranteed delivery features like TCP does. With UDP, packets are sent individually and are checked for integrity only if they arrive, and if they don't arrive then that's just the way it goes! But since it doesn't have to deal with all the error recovery, handshake, and acknowledgment procedures, it's a much faster protocol. UDP connections are used for things such as media streaming, VPN connections, VoIP, DNS, and NTP.

Internet Layer Protocols
The purpose of the Internet Layer is to provide routing, traffic control, addressing, and provide a network interface to the upper layers.

- **IP** – IP, or the Internet Protocol, is aware of the interconnected networks and provides routing based on the packet's address and routing tables. It's also responsible for choosing the best path to get the packet to its destination. IP receives segments from the Transport Layer, fragments them into packets, and then reassembles the packets back into segments on the receiving end. Each packet has the address of the sender and receiver.

- **ICMP** – The Internet Control Message Protocol is used as a messaging service for IP and does things such as provide information about certain network problems. Most people know ICMP because of the ping command, which uses an ICMP echo request to check for connectivity between network devices. This comes in handy since the Internet Protocol is not completely reliable. Traceroute (or tracert for Windows) uses ICMP as well.

- **IGMP** - The Internet Group Management Protocol is used between hosts and multicast routers on a single physical network to establish the host's membership in particular multicast groups. Multicasting allows one computer to send data to multiple computers that are set to accept content from the sending computer. IGMP only applies to IPv4 groups, and IGMPv3 is the latest version. IPv6 multicast groups will use Multicast Listener Discovery (MLD).

- **ARP** – The Address Resolution Protocol is used to find a MAC address (or hardware address) from a host where it knows its IP address. So, in other words, it's kind of like DNS for addresses where it "resolves" or maps an IP address to a MAC address. Computers have an ARP look up table which contains information about what IP addresses are associated with what MAC addresses. If an address is not found in this table, then the computer will send a broadcast using ARP asking what device has the IP address it is trying to resolve.

Link Layer Protocols

The purpose of the Link Layer is to define networking methods used within the local network link and its locally attached hosts. This layer also specifies hardware requirements for data transmission. The protocols used in this layer depend on what hardware is being used on the network. Some people say that ARP belongs here rather than the Internet layer. You will also hear that the Neighbor Discovery Protocol (NDP) goes here. NDP is similar to ARP, but for IPv6.

The bottom line when it comes to layers and protocols is that different authorities have different options on what protocols go where and even on the names of the TCP\IP model layers themselves. I would recommend going by whatever standard is used by the test or certification you are studying for.

Network Address Translation (NAT)

During your studies of IP addresses and routing you will more than likely encounter the concept of Network Address Translation and will need to know what it does and how it works.

NAT was originally intended to be used to help slow down the depletion of IP addresses by allowing multiple private (internal) IP addresses to be represented by less or even one public (external) IP address(es). Nowadays NAT is commonly used in corporate and even home networks to allow a large number of computers to communicate on the Internet with only one public IP address. Even your home router uses a form of NAT to allow all your devices Internet access without the need for public IP addresses on those devices. This comes in especially handy when companies have to pay a lot of money to have their own unique public IP addresses and have many more internal computers that need public access than they have public addresses for.

NAT usually takes place on your router or device that connects to the public Internet. There are three different types of NAT that you should know about, and each one serves a different purpose and uses your IP addresses differently.

- **Dynamic NAT** – Dynamic NAT is a many to many configuration where you map internal IP addresses to external IP addresses that are stored in a pool of available IP addresses. Dynamic NAT uses Port Address Translation (PAT),

- where the router assigns the internal client a port number to be used with the IP address so the packets are sent to the right computer. This is needed because multiple internal computers are sharing the same external or public IP address at the same time. This doesn't require a manual mapping on your router, but you do need to make sure you have enough external IP addresses to map to the internal IP addresses that require them.

- **Static NAT** – Static NAT is a one to one configuration where an internal IP address is mapped to a specific external IP address. This process is done manually, and once again you need to make sure you have enough external IP addresses to map to your internal IP addresses. This is used when you have more than one public IP address and want the mapping to stay consistent and not change. As you can see in figure 6.2, we have four internal (private) IP addresses statically mapped to four external (public) IP addresses. This information is kept in the NAP mapping table in the router. Any changes need to be made by hand.

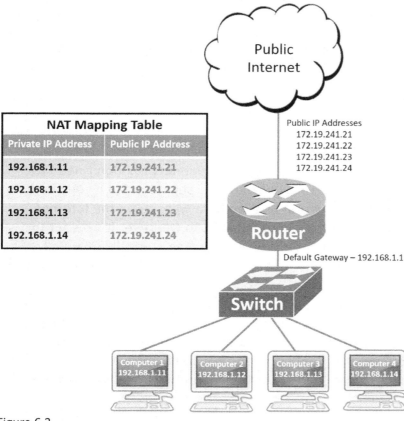

Figure 6.2

71

- **Overloading** – Overloading NAT is a one to many mapping where many internal IP addresses are mapped to one external IP address. This is the most commonly used type of NAT, and what your home router uses to allow all of your devices access to the Internet. Overloading is also known as PAT (Port Address Translation) because it uses different source ports to distinguish what data was from what internal network device. (Ports will be discussed later in this chapter.) NAT uses a naming convention for each address used in its process.

- **Inside local** – This is the internal source host address before any NAT translation occurs.

- **Outside local** – This is the address of an outside host as it appears to the internal network. This is usually the address of the router or other device that connects directly to the Internet.

- **Inside global** – This is the source address after the NAT translation process is used to get to the Internet.

- **Outside global** – This is the address of the outside destination, which would be the Internet.

Routing Protocols

In order to get our data from one network to another, it will need to be routed via a router or layer 3 switch. Remember that hosts on the same network don't need to route any traffic if it's not going outside of its own network segment. But if you need to reach a computer on a different network, or even hit a website on the Internet, that traffic will need to be routed out from your network to wherever it's meant to go to. I mentioned routing tables in Chapter 2 where you can statically (manually) enter routes so that your router knows where to send traffic that comes into its interfaces.

But who wants to do a bunch of manual labor on a bunch of routers? Static routing can become tedious really quickly, and there's also room for mistakes to be made. This is where dynamic routing and routing protocols come into play. Routing protocols use various methods to track routes and update routing tables so you don't need to do any of the work yourself.

Routing protocols allow routers to communicate with each other so they can forward traffic appropriately. These protocols use things such as route management, path determination, and discovery to get data from its source to its intended destination. There are many routing protocols you can use, but some are way more popular than others because they do a more efficient job of routing, and those are the ones I will go over in this section.

Before I begin with the protocols themselves, I want to go over the three classes of routing protocols. Then I will discuss what routing protocols are used within each class.

- **Link state** – Link state protocols use tables to keep track of directly attached neighbors or nodes and have a complete picture of the network topology. Each node constructs a map of the connectivity to the network, showing which nodes are connected to which other nodes. The state of the nodes are also kept track of. Triggered updates containing link state information are sent out as needed. Link state protocols use what they call Shortest Path First (SPF) to send data to its destination using the shortest number of hops. Link state routers are updated from all the routers in the entire network by passing information from router to nearest router. If a link is reported as down, then a different link will be used instead.

- **Distance vector** – Distance vector protocols use distance as their measurement calculations. Each time a packet goes through a router it counts as a hop, and the route with the least amount of hops is considered to be the best route. Some distance vector protocols also take into account network latency and bandwidth rather than only hop count. This protocol routinely sends its neighboring routers copies of its routing tables to keep them up to date. This is the simplest type of routing protocol.

- **Advanced distance vector** - Advanced distance vector protocols use aspects of both link state and distance vector protocols. They can discover neighbors and form relationships with them as well as distance vector methods to route traffic.

Now that we have an understanding of the routing classes, let's talk about the routing protocols themselves. I will go over the three most commonly used routing protocols:

- **(RIP) Routing Information Protocol** – RIP is a distance vector routing protocol and relies on hop count to figure out the best way to get to a remote network. It does, however, have a maximum hop count of fifteen, so if it can't make it to the remote network after fifteen hops, then it considers it unreachable.

With RIP, the routers exchange network reachability information with their nearest neighbors. It keeps things updated by sending out the entire routing table every thirty seconds. RIP is good for small networks, but that's about it. RIPv2 is the latest version, and has improvements over RIPv1 such as the ability to send subnet mask information with its route updates.

- **(OSPF) Open Shortest Path First** – OSPF is a link state routing protocol, and the routers exchange topology information with their nearest neighbors. Its job is to find the best path for packets as they pass through connected networks. The main benefit of OSPF is that it knows about the entire network topology and can make decisions based on that knowledge.

- **(EIGRP) Enhanced Interior Gateway Routing Protocol** – EIGRP is an advanced distance vector routing protocol that allows routers to exchange topology information, but still uses distance vector methods such as bandwidth, delay, and reliability to make decisions for forwarding traffic.

Routing Tables

As I mentioned earlier in the book, routing tables are databases stored in RAM that contain information about directly connected networks. These tables can be updated and maintained dynamically by routing protocols or statically. These tables will keep track of information such as the network address assigned to interfaces, subnet masks, route sources, destination network, and the outgoing interface.

Routing tables contain a list of IP addresses, and each address in the list identifies a remote router (or gateway) that the local router is configured to know about. These tables are basically used for the router to find the next hop towards the destination network. Routing tables are used differently by routing protocols (dynamic) compared to when you create your own routing table by hand (static).

If you take a look at figure 6.3, you can see how complicated routing tables can get if you had to manage them yourself. In this example, the table only has two fields, the network and the next hop, which is the next interface that the data would go through to reach its destination. In the real world there would be many more computers on each network and switches involved, so things would be way complex.

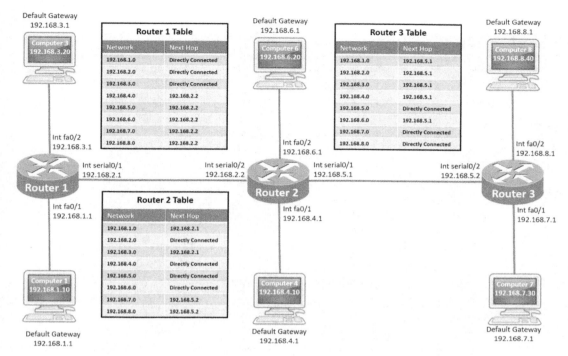

Figure 6.3

Your computer keeps a routing table of its own that it uses to find other networks to send data to. If you are running Microsoft Windows, you can open a command prompt and type in **route print** to have it bring up your local routing table (figure 6.3). The **netstat –rn** command will do the same thing, and will also work for Linux as well.

Figure 6.3

There are 5 sections in the Windows routing table, and here is what they are for:

- **Network Destination** – Shows the networks segments that the computer is or has connected to.
- **Netmask** – Lists the subnet mask of the segment itself.
- **Gateway** – Used to determine which destination network it needs to send the packet to.
- **Interface** – Tells the computer which network interface is connected to the appropriate destination network.

- **Metric** – Tells the computer the cost of the route (as in how long it will take to get there or how reliable the path is). It's only used if there is more than one path to a network.

Ports

The last topic I want to go over for this chapter is network ports. Port numbers are used by TCP and UDP to keep track of different communications passing through the network at the same time. A port is a logical entity that identifies a specific process or a type of network service. These port numbers are associated with the IP address of the host and the protocol in use. So, if you are running more than one instance of the same network service on your computer, it will use different port numbers to keep your sessions separated.

There are many port numbers that can be used for network services, and in fact they start at 0 and go all the way up to 65,535. Port numbers are either assigned by the operating system as needed, or are configured manually to work with specific applications or services. Ports 0 to 1,023 are considered well-known ports. Ports 1,024 to 49,151 are registered ports used by software developers to use with their specific application. Ports 49,152 to 65,535 are ports available to be used by the public.

Many commonly used programs are assigned their own specific port numbers to assure reliable communication and ease of configuration since there is a standard number or numbers to use. Here is a listing of some of the most commonly used applications or services and their assigned port numbers (figure 6.4). You should recognize many of these protocols from our earlier discussion.

Port Number	Protocol	Description
20 & 21	FTP (File Transfer Protocol)	Used to transfer files between computers over the network or the Internet.
22	SSH (Secure Shell)	A secure method to access devices via a command line over the network or Internet.
23	Telnet	Similar to SSH but not secure.
25	SMTP (Simple Mail Transfer Protocol)	Used to send email from a mail server to a user's mailbox.
53	DNS (Domain Name System)	Translates names to IP addresses on networks and the Internet.
67 & 68	DHCP (Dynamic Host Configuration Protocol)	Used to assign IP addresses to DHCP enabled devices so they can communicate on the network.
69	TFTP (Trivial File Transfer Protocol)	An unsecure version of FTP.
80	HTTP (Hypertext Transfer Protocol)	The protocol used to access web pages on the Internet.
110	POP3 (Post Office Protocol version 3)	One of the older protocols used to retrieve email from email servers.
119	NNTP (Network News Transport Protocol)	Used for transporting Usenet news articles to NNTP clients.
123	NTP (Network Time Protocol)	Keeps devices on the network synchronized in regards to their time.
143	IMAP4 (Internet Message Access Protocol)	A more robust protocol used to retrieve email from email servers.
161 & 162	SNMP (Simple Network Management Protocol)	Provides the ability for administrators to monitor and configure SNMP enabled devices remotely.
389	LDAP (Lightweight Directory Access Protocol)	Allows for access distributed directory information.
443	HTTPS (Secure Hypertext Transfer Protocol)	Provides a secure connection to websites using SSL or TLS.
993	IMAP4 over SSL	Allows for the use of IMAP4 over secure connections.
995	POP3 over SSL	Allows for the use of POP3 over secure connections.
3389	RDP (Remote Desktop Protocol)	Used by Windows Terminal Server for remote desktop connections.

Figure 6.4

You might have seen a URL that had a port number "assigned" to it and not realized what it was. For example, the URL **http://webserver.com:8080** tells your computer to use port 8080 rather than the default of 80 for this URL.

Chapter 7 – The Internet

If there's one thing about networking that everyone knows, it's how to use the world's biggest network, the Internet. Actually the Internet is a network consisting of other networks that are connected together, making universal communication possible. The Internet is not owned by any one person or corporation, which makes it possible to grow and expand into a larger entity. Sure, there are governing bodies that control the standards of communication, and that's a good thing to make sure that all these individual networks get along with each other.

History

Back in the 1960s, ARPANET (Advanced Research Projects Agency Network) started experimenting with packet switched networking while working on a project for the Department of Defense (DoD), which, if you remember, has their TCP\IP Model that I discussed in Chapter 6. The initial purpose of this network was a way for government personnel to share information with each other during times of war. In 1969, ARPANET delivered its first message using node to node communication from one computer to another. Then, in the 1970s, this technology was expanded with the development of TCP\IP, which set standards for how data could be transmitted between multiple networks.

ARPANET adopted TCP\IP in 1983, and began working on what they called "the network of networks", which eventually became the Internet. This is not to be confused with the World Wide Web, which came about in 1989. The World Wide Web is an information sharing space that uses URLs and hyperlinks to connect content and information to other sources of information. Think of the World Wide Web as what you access with your web browser rather than it being the Internet in itself. And in 1992, students and researchers at the University of Illinois developed the first web browser called Mosaic, which eventually became to be known as Netscape. Now we have multiple browsers and use the Internet for all sorts of things such as streaming video, conference calls, FTP file transfers, VPN connections, and so on.

How the Internet Works

The Internet is a global network of computers and other devices that are connected by multiple networks run by many different people and organizations. Going back to our discussion of IP addresses, each device that is publicly reachable on the Internet must have its own unique IP address. Now don't confuse this with internal computers that are reachable via NAT translation, because they still use an externally translated public IP address for Internet communication. If you have a broadband Internet connection at home, your modem is using a public IP address to connect to the Internet.

The Internet backbone is made up of many larger networks or network service providers who have the resources to handle large amounts of data on their networks. Think of a backbone as the main pipe or core that does all the heavy lifting. Branching off these network service providers are regional ISPs and then local ISPs, with all types of routers and other network equipment in use between them.

Many of the Application Layer protocols that I went over from the last chapter are used over the Internet, including HTTP, HTTPS, DNS, Telnet, SSH, FTP, and so on. Some of them you most likely don't even know you are using, such as DNS, which you use every time you type in a website address into your web browser. You might remember that DNS resolves host names to their associated IP addresses so you don't have to remember the IP addresses of computers on the network or websites on the Internet.

DNS Root Servers

And speaking of DNS, you might or might not know that there are DNS root servers used on the Internet to resolve queries for the all the top level domains. These servers handle queries for records stored within the root zone, and can also refer other requests to the appropriate Top Level Domain server.

So when you go to a website that ends in .com, .net, .edu, .org, etc., they are handled by their respective top level DNS servers. There are many public top level domains than you would ever care to keep track of. Most countries have their own domain as well, such as .us for the United States and .au for Australia. These domains are organized into levels with sub-levels within each top level domain. Figure 7.1 shows a simplified version of the public Internet domain structure with just a few of the many domains and how at the very top of the domain levels is the root domain which is represented by a dot or period ".". Then you have the top level domains such as .com, and within them you have the second level domains such as Google, which would be google.com when you put it all together.

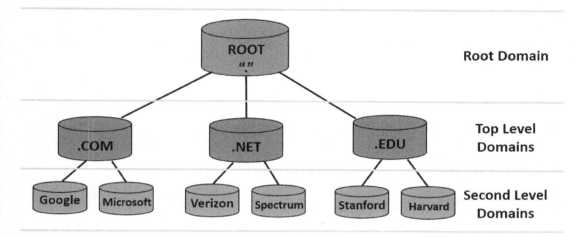

Figure 7.1

There are thirteen root servers that each have a current copy of the DNS root zone. These servers may be responsible for taking care of DNS business on the Internet, but that doesn't mean there are only thirteen physical servers doing all the work! The thirteen IP addresses associated with the root servers are actually accessed by many servers that are spread out geographically. These thirteen root servers are managed by twelve independent organizations, and the physical servers are spread throughout the world. Figure 7.2 shows all the root server names and who they are managed by.

Windows DNS servers, and most likely other DNS servers, keep a listing of all the root server names and IP addresses to make it easier to perform their queries when trying to resolve names to IP addresses.

Root Server Name	Managed By
a.root-servers.net	VeriSign, Inc.
b.root-servers.net	University of Southern California
c.root-servers.net	Cogent Communications
d.root-servers.net	University of Maryland
e.root-servers.net	NASA
f.root-servers.net	Internet Systems Consortium, Inc.
g.root-servers.net	US Department of Defense
h.root-servers.net	US Army
i.root-servers.net	Netnod
j.root-servers.net	VeriSign, Inc.
k.root-servers.net	RIPE NCC
l.root-servers.net	ICANN
m.root-servers.net	WIDE

Figure 7.2

Using the Internet as a WAN

So far our discussion has been with local networks, or LANs (Local Area Networks), but we are not limited by distance these days thanks to the Internet and the fast connections we have almost any place we happen to be. With today's global economy comes the need to expand networks beyond the office building and into other cities, states, and even countries. This is where a WAN, or Wide Area Network, comes into play.

There are a couple of ways you can use the Internet as a WAN, and it is by connecting remote offices together so they function as one network, and then using cloud resources to run your organization so the cloud service is providing all the resources (such as storage and compute power) to run your servers.

Remote Office

If you have an office in another part of town or even outside of town, it's possible to connect to that office over a dedicated leased line, which is usually from a phone or cable Internet provider. It will be a point to point permanently connected line that you will pay a monthly charge to use, and it's usually not cheap with things like speed and distance between sites affecting the cost. You might have heard older terms like T1 or DS3 lines, which are still in use today. Now we also have Ethernet WAN and MPLS (Multiprotocol Label Switching) technologies that provide improved performance. Don't confuse a leased line with regular broadband because broadband connections don't provide the dedicated connections that leased lines do.

Once you get your leased line configured, then you can use your remote site as if it were another network segment on your local network. This comes in handy for setting up things like a remote backup location or a disaster recovery site so if the main office goes down you can carry on with business at your other location.

Cloud Services

The latest trend in IT management is to house your network services in the cloud and access them via your Internet connection. The term "cloud" refers to having another company host resources like storage or email on their servers that are then made available for you to access for a monthly fee.

Some companies use the cloud to run things like application servers or domain controllers so they don't need to buy the expensive hardware and have someone manage it in house. Plus, the cloud provider can offer backup services for the servers themselves as well as the data contained on them.

You can also use the cloud for shared storage rather than doing it locally, and that way you can access your storage from anywhere you have Internet access. There are even services like DropBox and Microsoft OneDrive that home users can take advantage of for cloud storage.

The latest trend taking hold is to utilize Software as a Service (or SaaS). This is where you have subscriptions to the software you use rather than buying it and installing it locally. One well known example of SaaS is Microsoft Office 365, where you use programs like Word and Excel online via a web browser rather than installing Office on your local computer.

Other cloud based computing options include Infrastructure as a Service (IaaS) where you are using resources like servers (as virtual machines) and networking resources in the cloud rather than on site. There is also Platform as a Service (PaaS) which is used to supply an environment to run your applications and can be used to assist with software development. Some of the top cloud service providers are Amazon Web Services (AWS), Microsoft Azure, and Google Cloud.

Virtual Private Networks (VPN)
One last topic I want to discuss when it comes to using the Internet as a network is the process of connecting to your network using a VPN or Virtual Private Network. Unfortunately, many people get stuck working after hours these days, but thanks to VPNs, they can put in their overtime from the comfort of their own home. A VPN is used to make a secure connection from their home or other location directly to their work either into the network itself or directly to a specific computer. This way they can use their home (or remote) computer as if it was actually on the network at the office, or they can do a remote connection to their actual work computer on their desk.

The VPN connection is accomplished by making a dedicated secure tunnel through the internet from the remote location to the destination location. The traffic is encrypted, so anyone intercepting it will not be able to read it. When it comes to types of VPNs, most people use a remote access VPN, where you have client software running on the remote computer and you connect into your corporate firewall with a username and password which allows you access to the network. From there you can either have unrestricted access to the network, or be restricted to accessing one or more individual computers or other resources. Another type is a site to site VPN, where the connection is always up and running allowing one or more user from the remote site access to the other site. This type of connection can be either one way or both ways depending on your needs.

For the VPN clients, you will use the one that matches the type of firewall you will be connected to at the remote site. Common brands are Cisco, Checkpoint, Palo Alto Juniper, and SonicWall. You can also set up Windows and Linux servers to act as firewalls for VPN access if you don't want to invest in an actual hardware firewall. Some network routers can also have VPN functionality built-in, and there are also other VPN web-based services like SecureLink that will use appliances at the corporate site and the VPN connection will be initiated via a web browser.

Chapter 8 – Windows Networking

Since Microsoft Windows is the world's most popular operating system and most likely what you will be using at home and in the office, I figured it was a good idea to dedicate a chapter on Windows networking. Yes, I know there are plenty of Mac and Linux geeks out there as well, but let's face it, many non-Windows users are pretty technical to begin with, especially Linux users.

You may recall in Chapter 1 that I talked about peer-to-peer and client-server networking as well as Workgroups and Domains, but I want to expand on that a little bit more in this chapter.

Workgroups vs. Domains
When it comes to configuring networking in Windows, you will either set up your computers to be in a workgroup, or to join an Active Directory domain. For your home network you will most likely use a workgroup, and for the office you will most likely configure a domain unless it's small enough (10 or less computers) to where you can get by with a workgroup.

Workgroups
Workgroups are used when there is no centralized administration needed and every computer is an equal member of the workgroup. You configure your resource sharing on each computer and only users who have accounts on a particular computer can access that computer either locally or remotely. This can get complicated if you have a lot of users that need to access multiple computers over the network because you will need to configure user accounts and permissions on each computer they need to access. It's usually a good idea to designate one or two computers for shared resources, and then just configure the user accounts on those computers.

 If you are wondering what happened to the Windows Homegroup network sharing feature, it was removed in one of the Windows 10 major updates, so we are now back to just Workgroups.

To check and\or change the name of your workgroup (and also your computer name), you will need to go to the Windows system settings and look under the section that says Computer name, domain, and workgroup settings (figure 8.1).

Computer names are very important with Windows networking, since the computer name is most likely what you will be using to search for and access network resources with (unless you feel like doing it the hard way by remembering their IP addresses!).

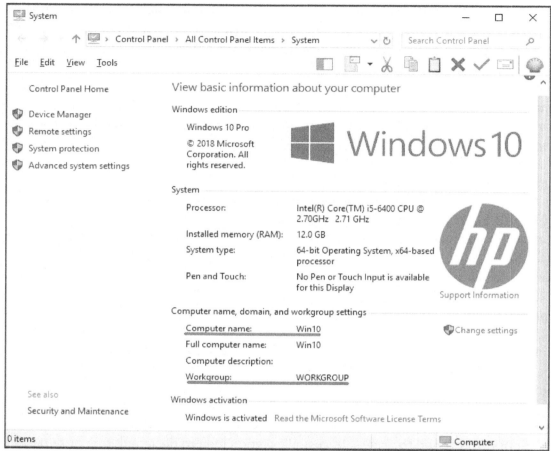

Figure 8.1

To get to the Windows system settings you can type in **system** in the search box or in Cortana and open the System properties box as shown in figure 8.1. Next to the word *Workgroup* will be the workgroup name. (In my example it's called WORKGROUP.) If your computer was joined to a domain, it would say *domain* rather than *Workgroup* in this section.

If the workgroup names don't all match, then you will need to change them so they do. From the same screen in figure 8.1, simply click on the link that says *Change settings* and you will be presented with a box that looks similar to figure 8.2. From here you will click on the button that says *Change*, and then type in the new name for the workgroup. You can also change the computer name from here at the same time. Keep in mind you will have to reboot the computer for the changes to take effect.

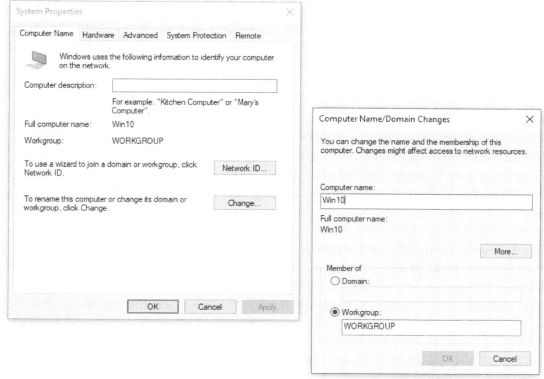

Figure 8.2

Another thing you should check for when using a workgroup is to make sure every computer that you want to be a part of the workgroup is on the same subnet. Check the IP addresses of each one to make sure they are configured correctly. If you are using something like your wireless router for a DHCP server to give out IP addresses, then you are most likely going to be okay with your IP configuration.

Once you have the workgroup name, computer names, and IP addresses figured out, then you will need to create the user accounts for the people who will be active users on your network. This can be done from the Windows Control Panel, and you can create standard users and users with administrator rights.

Standard user accounts are for people who need to do everyday tasks on the computer such as run programs, go online, print, and so on. Standard users can also install and uninstall certain software as well. It's usually a good idea to make everyone on your network a standard user, and then if they need something done that requires higher privileges, they can have an administrator do it.

Administrator user accounts have full control over the computer and can do things such as install or uninstall any software, add or remove user accounts, add or remove hardware, and make changes that affect Windows itself. If you are logged in as a standard user and need to do something that requires administrator access, many times you will be prompted to enter the username and password of an administrator, so you don't need to actually log out and then back in as an administrator to get the job done.

Domains

If you work at a company with a reasonable amount of computers that run Windows, then you are most likely part of a Windows Active Directory domain. In a domain, all access and security is controlled by centralized servers called domain controllers, and all the permissions and other policy settings are kept in the Active Directory database.

You log into your computer with your domain username and password and that determines what level of access you have to all network resources like file servers and printers. Using domains makes it easy for network administrators to control user accounts and permissions since it can all be done from one place and applied to the entire network.

With an Active Directory domain comes the ability to create and apply Group Policies to users and computers. These policies are used to do things such as automatically assign network printers, prevent users from changing computer settings, and install software automatically, as well as change thousands of other settings.

If you are curious about what kind of policy changes you can make using Group Policy, then open the local policy editor on your computer to see similar settings. Just search for and run **gpedit.msc** from the Start button search box. (It won't be available on the Home versions of Windows though.)

Resource Sharing and Permissions

No matter what type of network configuration you are configuring, you should come up with a plan on what users will have what type of access to your shared resources. Permissions need to be set properly, otherwise you will have users who are able to access things they shouldn't and users who will be blocked from using resources they should be able to use.

For files and folder sharing and permissions you can right click on the item you want to share, and then choose *Properties*. From there you will need to assign share level permissions and then Security (or NTFS) permissions. Share permissions are what you use to have the resource be shared on the network for other users to access. Security permissions are the levels of access you can give to those users who are allowed to use the shared resources. Just keep in mind that when share and NTFS permissions are used simultaneously, the most restrictive permission will always apply. Also know that NTFS permissions apply to users who are logged on to the server locally (and over the network), while share permissions don't because you are not accessing a shared resource while logged on locally to the server that hosts that share. Here is a summary of the share and NTFS permissions available on a Windows network. These apply to workgroups and domains.

Below is a summary of the share and NTFS permissions you can assign to your resources. Figure 8.3 shows the permissions screens for each one.

Share Permissions

- **Read** - Users can view file and folder names, open files, and run programs. The *Everyone* group is assigned *Read* permissions by default.

- **Change** - Users can do everything allowed by the *Read* permission, as well as add files and subfolders, edit files, and delete subfolders and files.

- **Full Control** - Users can do everything allowed by the *Read* and *Change* permissions, as well as change permissions for NTFS files and folders only. The *Administrators* group is granted a *Full Control* permission by default.

NTFS Permissions

- **Full Control** - Users can add, modify, move, and delete files and directories, as well as their associated properties. Users can also change permissions for all files and subdirectories.

- **Modify** - Users can view and modify files and their properties, including adding files to or deleting files from a directory, or file properties to or from a file.

- **Read & Execute** - Users can run executable files, including scripts, as well as open files.

- **Read** - Users can open files, and view file properties and directories.

- **Write** - Users can write to a file as well as create files and folders.

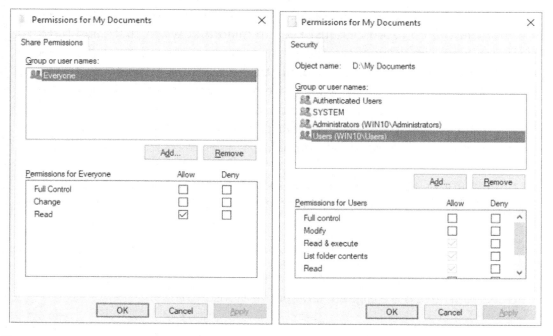

Figure 8.3

Windows Firewall

When working with Windows networking you will still need to account for security measures and realize that Windows computers will not just let any traffic pass from computer to computer without being checked. If it did allow everything through unfiltered, then Microsoft wouldn't have much of a reputation for being a secure operating system.

Windows comes with a built-in software firewall that is designed to filter incoming and outgoing traffic on your computer to help the overall security of your computer. For the most part it's something you won't really need to mess with, and you can usually just let it do its job in the background. But if you need to allow or deny a certain application or service, then you can do it from the firewall. For example, you may come across a situation where a Windows computer on your network is not pingable, and it can be a case of the firewall blocking ICMP traffic. In this case you can go into the firewall and allow it so you are able to ping the computer. (I will be discussing the ping command later in this chapter.)

To open the Windows Firewall you can do so from Control Panel, or simply type in firewall in the Start menu search box to open the firewall application. As you can see in figure 8.4, the Windows Firewall is divided up into different panes that show you certain types of information and also allows you to make configuration changes.

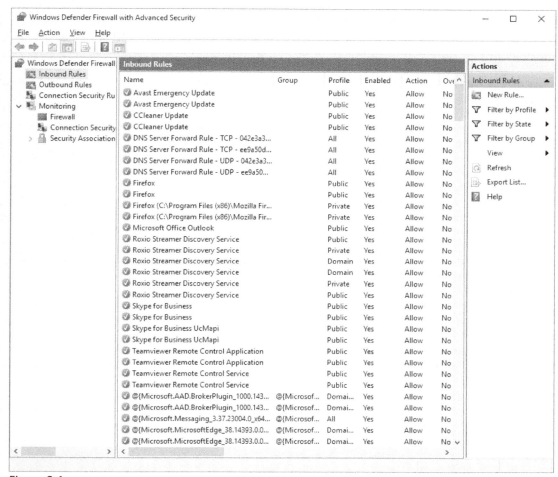

Figure 8.4

On the left side you have your inbound and outbound rules which are used to control what comes into your computer over the network or Internet and what your computer is sending out over the network. The Connection Security Rules section is where you can create a custom rule that determines how computers are authenticated using IPsec. IPsec (Internet Protocol Security) is a framework of standards for ensuring private, secure communications over IP networks. The Monitoring section is where you can see stats on how the firewall is working as well as setup things like notifications and configure logging options.

The middle pane shows things like your inbound and outbound rules depending on what you click on from the pane on the left. So, if you were to click on Inbound Rules on the left, it would show you all of the rules for incoming traffic in the middle pane like figure 8.4 shows. You can then do things from the right pane such as disable the rule or copy it to create a new rule from the existing rule settings. If you click on *Properties* (figure 8.5), it will show you a bunch of information relating to that rule, such as what program it applies to, the protocols and ports it uses, what IP addresses it applies to, and so on.

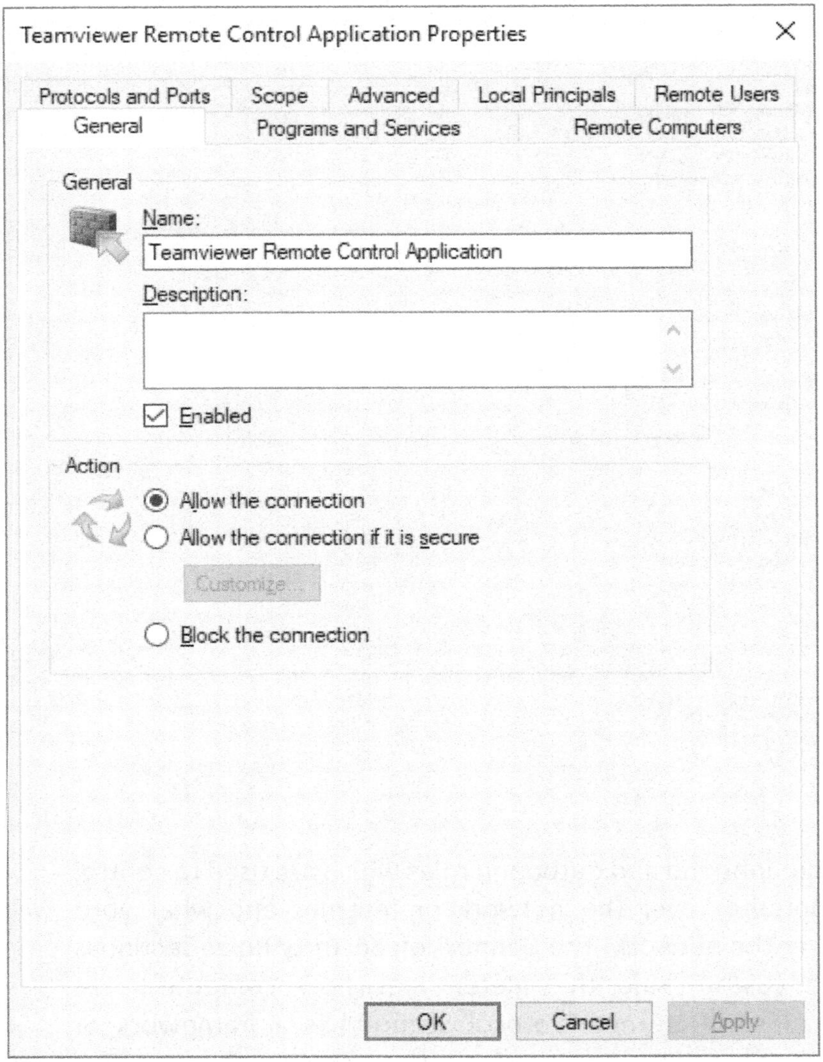

Figure 8.5

To make a new rule you would first click on *Inbound Rules* or *Outbound Rules* (depending on which direction you want the rule to apply to) and then click on *New Rule* in the right pane. Then you will have to choose if the rule applies to a program, port, predefined Windows experience, or a custom rule (figure 8.6). The rule type that you choose will determine what configuration steps you will need to perform next will be.

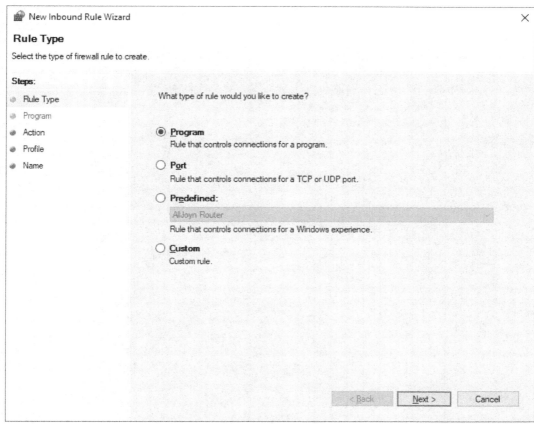

Figure 8.6

If you ever need to see if the Windows Firewall is responsible for blocking a network application or traffic, you can disable it to do some testing. You can do so by clicking on the *Action* menu and then click on *Properties*.

IPconfig Command

I talked about the IPconfig command a little in Chapter 4, but want to bring it up again because you will be using it a lot if you plan on networking with Windows-based computers. Also remember that the **ifconfig** command is what you will be using for Unix and Linux.

The **ipconfig** command has various options (called switches) that you can use to get specific information about you IP configuration. Some are more useful than others, and some are meant for more advanced troubleshooting. I will go over the ones that are most commonly used by your average network administrator, or even home users. To get to the help section that shows the switches and examples, type in **ipconfig /?** and press enter.

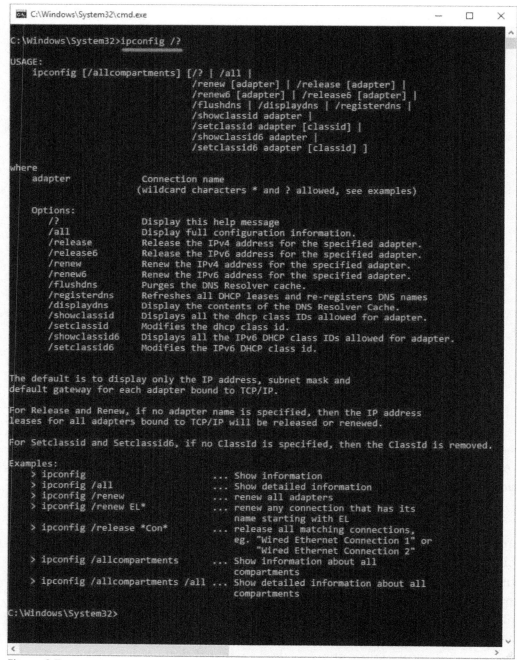

Figure 8.7

I discussed how you can use the **/all** switch to find out more detailed information about your IP address configuration such as the host name, DHCP server address, and MAC address. If you need to get a different IP address via DHCP for some reason, you can use the **/release** and **/renew** switches where **/release** will drop the IP address from your network adapter, and the **/renew** switch will have the DHCP service go out and contact the DHCP server to get another IP address. Keep in mind that a lot of the time you will end up with the same IP address if it's still available.

The **/displaydns** switch will show you the entries in your DNS resolver cache, which stores DNS information about hosts that you have resolved online and on the network, as well as any entries stored in your local hosts file. Running this command will most likely scroll a very long list of entries, so you can press **Ctrl-C** to stop the command from running. You can always pipe the command to **more** to get one page at a time. The command to do that would look like this ipconfig **/displaydns | more**. Then you would press the spacebar to get to the next page or enter to get to the next line.

The **/flushdns** command is used to clear out the contents of the DNS resolver cache. You may encounter an issue where you are trying to access a network resource or website that has had its name changed and your computer is still trying to resolve it to the old name. This is where flushing your DNS cache is handy because it will clear out all that old information as well as any other DNS information it has stored.

The last switch we will discuss is the **/registerdns** switch which will register your computer with your DNS server. When your computer is first brought online on a network, it is supposed to register itself with your DNS server. Sometimes this doesn't work for some reason, or if you rename your computer you might want to re-register it with your DNS server. This is where the **/registerdns** command comes in handy.

As you can see, the **ipconfig** command is a useful tool for network troubleshooting and diagnostics, and you can obtain a lot of useful information if you use the right switches to do so.

Network Utilities
There are several tools and utilities you can use to help troubleshoot and configure your network settings, and the more tools you have in your tool belt, the better. I will go over some of the built-in Windows tools and then talk about other third party utilities you can use when you are having network issues.

Ping

Ping (Packet Internet Groper) is a program used to test whether a particular network host is online by sending an ICMP (Internet control message protocol) echo request and waiting for a response. It is used for troubleshooting connectivity between network devices such as servers, routers, workstations, and printers. It is one of the most commonly used tools used to troubleshoot network connectivity between devices.

You can ping a host from a command prompt simply by typing **ping** followed by the IP address. For example, type **ping 192.168.0.1** to see if the host with the 192.168.0.1 IP address is reachable. It also works with hostnames on the same network, so if you have a server called WebServer you can type in **ping WebServer** to check for connectivity (assuming DNS is configured correctly so it can resolve the name to its IP address). You can also ping a website by typing ping www.microsoft.com to check its availability. For Windows computers, you will need to allow ICMP packets through the firewall in order to be able to ping those computers.

To use the PING utility simply open a command prompt from your Start menu or type in cmd from your run command box or your search box.

When a PING is successful you get a reply back from the host showing its IP address and other information such as the time it took for the reply to go through (figure 8.8).

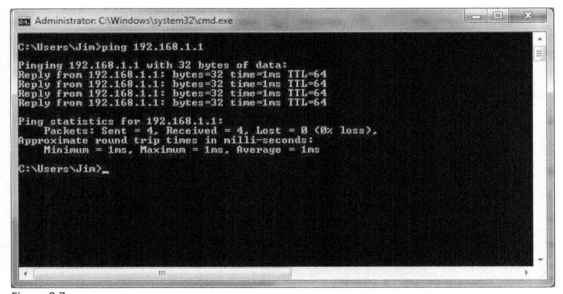

Figure 8.7

When a ping response is not successful, you can get a variety of error replies. Here are the main error messages and what they mean.

- **TTL Expired in Transit** - The TTL value determines the maximum amount of time an IP packet may live in the network without reaching its destination. It is effectively bound on the number of routers an IP packet may pass through before being discarded. This message indicates that the TTL expired in transit. Number of required hops exceeds TTL. Increase TTL by using the **ping -i** switch.

- **Destination Host Unreachable** - The host that you are trying to ping is down or is not operating on the network. A local or remote route does not exist for destination host. Modify the local route table or notify the router administrator.

- **Request Timed Out** - The ping command timed out because there was no reply from the host. No Echo Reply messages were received due to network traffic, failure of the ARP request packet filtering, or router error. Increase the wait time using the **ping -w** switch.

- **Unknown Host** - The IP Address or the Host Name does not exist in the network or the destination host name cannot be resolved. Verify name and availability of DNS servers.

Tracert
Tracert (short for Trace Route) is a Windows version of the traceroute command used in other operating systems and is used to trace the path from one host to another. It sends a packet and then displays how many hops the packet took to reach the host and how long each hop took. It is a good way to find out where the connection is being broken, or if there is a bottleneck if you are having connection issues. You can use it for devices on your network as well as websites and other Internet resources. Just type tracert (figure 8.8) with the IP address, host name, or website name afterwards and it will show you the details as it makes its way to its destination, assuming it makes it!

```
C:\Windows\System32\cmd.exe                                          —    □    ×

Microsoft Windows [Version 10.0.17134.228]
(c) 2018 Microsoft Corporation. All rights reserved.

C:\Windows\System32>tracert www.onlinecomputertips.com

Tracing route to onlinecomputertips.com [50.62.101.145]
over a maximum of 30 hops:

  1      4 ms      4 ms      6 ms   192.168.0.1
  2     21 ms     17 ms     12 ms   142.254.183.193
  3     13 ms     17 ms     16 ms   agg62.simicacd01h.socal.rr.com [76.167.26.89]
  4     19 ms     21 ms     14 ms   agg23.vnnycajz01r.socal.rr.com [72.129.14.178]
  5     16 ms     17 ms     17 ms   agg29.lsancarc01r.socal.rr.com [72.129.13.0]
  6     16 ms     27 ms    107 ms   bu-ether16.atlngamq46w-bcr00.tbone.rr.com [66.109.6.92]
  7     25 ms     20 ms     26 ms   bu-ether45.chctilwc00w-bcr00.tbone.rr.com [107.14.19.36]
  8      *         *         *      Request timed out.
  9      *         *        27 ms   ae-2-23.bear1.Phoenix1.Level3.net [4.69.210.165]
 10     38 ms     32 ms     35 ms   4.16.137.146
 11     41 ms     29 ms     27 ms   be38.trmc0215-01.ars.mgmt.phx3.gdg [184.168.0.69]
 12     32 ms     27 ms     27 ms   be38.trmc0215-01.ars.mgmt.phx3.gdg [184.168.0.69]
 13     38 ms     28 ms     27 ms   ip-97-74-255-129.ip.secureserver.net [97.74.255.129]
 14     38 ms     27 ms     27 ms   ip-50-62-101-145.ip.secureserver.net [50.62.101.145]

Trace complete.

C:\Windows\System32>_
```

Figure 8.8

As you can see here it took fourteen hops to reach its destination with a time out in the middle. Just because you see a time out doesn't necessarily mean there was an issue with one of the hops.

PathPing

PathPing is similar to ping and tracert, and will send sends multiple echo request messages to each router or node as it travels to its destination over a period of time. Then it will calculate results based on the packets returned from each hop, showing any slowdown or packet loss along the way. This allows you to pinpoint which routers or links might the cause of your connectivity problem. To use PathPing simply open a command prompt and type **pathping** with the IP address, URL, or FQDN that you want to test connectivity to after it (figure 8.9).

```
C:\Windows\System32\cmd.exe                                          —     □     ✕

C:\Windows\System32>pathping www.onlinecomputertips.com

Tracing route to onlinecomputertips.com [50.62.101.145]
over a maximum of 30 hops:
  0  Win10 [192.168.0.2]
  1  192.168.0.1
  2  142.254.183.193
  3  agg62.simicacd01h.socal.rr.com [76.167.26.89]
  4  agg23.vnnycajz01r.socal.rr.com [72.129.14.178]
  5  agg29.lsancarc01r.socal.rr.com [72.129.13.0]
  6  bu-ether16.atlngamq46w-bcr00.tbone.rr.com [66.109.6.92]
  7  bu-ether45.chctilwc00w-bcr00.tbone.rr.com [107.14.19.36]
  8    *         *         *
Computing statistics for 175 seconds...
                Source to Here    This Node/Link
Hop  RTT       Lost/Sent = Pct   Lost/Sent = Pct  Address
  0                                                Win10 [192.168.0.2]
                                  0/ 100 =  0%     |
  1    5ms     0/ 100 =  0%       0/ 100 =  0%     192.168.0.1
                                  0/ 100 =  0%     |
  2   16ms     0/ 100 =  0%       0/ 100 =  0%     142.254.183.193
                                  0/ 100 =  0%     |
  3   19ms     0/ 100 =  0%       0/ 100 =  0%     agg62.simicacd01h.socal.rr.com [76.167.26.89
                                  0/ 100 =  0%     |
  4   22ms     0/ 100 =  0%       0/ 100 =  0%     agg23.vnnycajz01r.socal.rr.com [72.129.14.17
                                  0/ 100 =  0%     |
  5   21ms     0/ 100 =  0%       0/ 100 =  0%     agg29.lsancarc01r.socal.rr.com [72.129.13.0]
                                  0/ 100 =  0%     |
  6   22ms     0/ 100 =  0%       0/ 100 =  0%     bu-ether16.atlngamq46w-bcr00.tbone.rr.com [6
                                  0/ 100 =  0%     |
  7   25ms     0/ 100 =  0%       0/ 100 =  0%     bu-ether45.chctilwc00w-bcr00.tbone.rr.com [1

Trace complete.

C:\Windows\System32>
```

Figure 8.9

The results show the initial trace, and then it computes the statics of the trace to tell you the response time for each one of the hops and its success rate.

Netstat

Netstat will show you your active TCP connections and what ports are actively listening as well as other useful information. If you don't use any of the switches with the command then it will only display the active TCP connections. For example, if you use the **–e** switch then it will show you the Ethernet statistics for packets sent and received (figure 8.10).

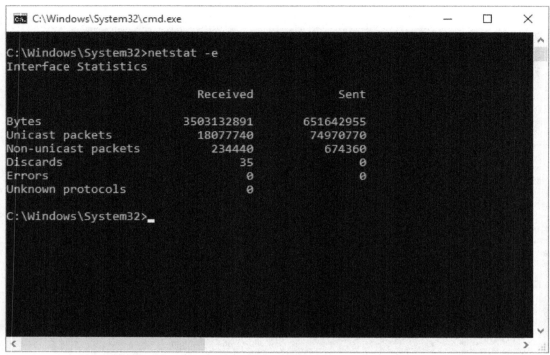

C:\Windows\System32\cmd.exe — □ ×

```
C:\Windows\System32>netstat -e
Interface Statistics

                          Received                Sent

Bytes                   3503132891           651642955
Unicast packets           18077740            74970770
Non-unicast packets         234440              674360
Discards                        35                   0
Errors                           0                   0
Unknown protocols                0

C:\Windows\System32>_
```

Figure 8.10

Here are the other switches you can use with the netstat command.

-a   Shows all connections and listening ports.

-b   Shows the executable involved in creating each connection or port.

-e   Shows Ethernet statistics.

-f   Shows the Fully Qualified Domain Names for foreign addresses.

-n   Shows addresses and port numbers in numerical form.

-o   Shows the owning process ID associated with each connection.

-p proto Shows connections for the protocol specified by proto.

-r   Shows the routing table.

-s   Shows per-protocol statistics.

-t   Shows the current connection offload state.

-v   When used along with **-b**, this will display the sequence of components involved in creating the connection or listening port for all executables.

NSlookup

NSlookup (Name Server Lookup) is used to query DNS to obtain domain names or IP addresses and their mapping, as well as diagnose DNS related problems. There are a variety of ways you can use NSlookup to perform various tasks, and I will go over some of the more common things you can do with the command.

If you run *nslookup domain name* you can find the IP address for that domain. So, if we type **nslookup microsoft.com** we get the result shown in figure 8.11 with the IP addresses of 104.215.95.187 and 52.164.206.56.

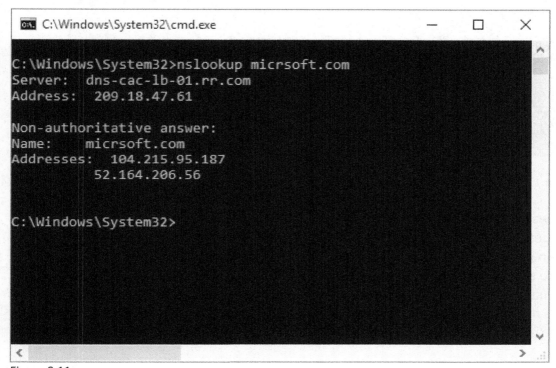

Figure 8.11

If we add the **type=ns** switch to the same command it will show us their name servers or DNS servers. So, typing in **nslookup -type=ns micrsoft.com** gives us the result in figure 8.12, showing four different name servers.

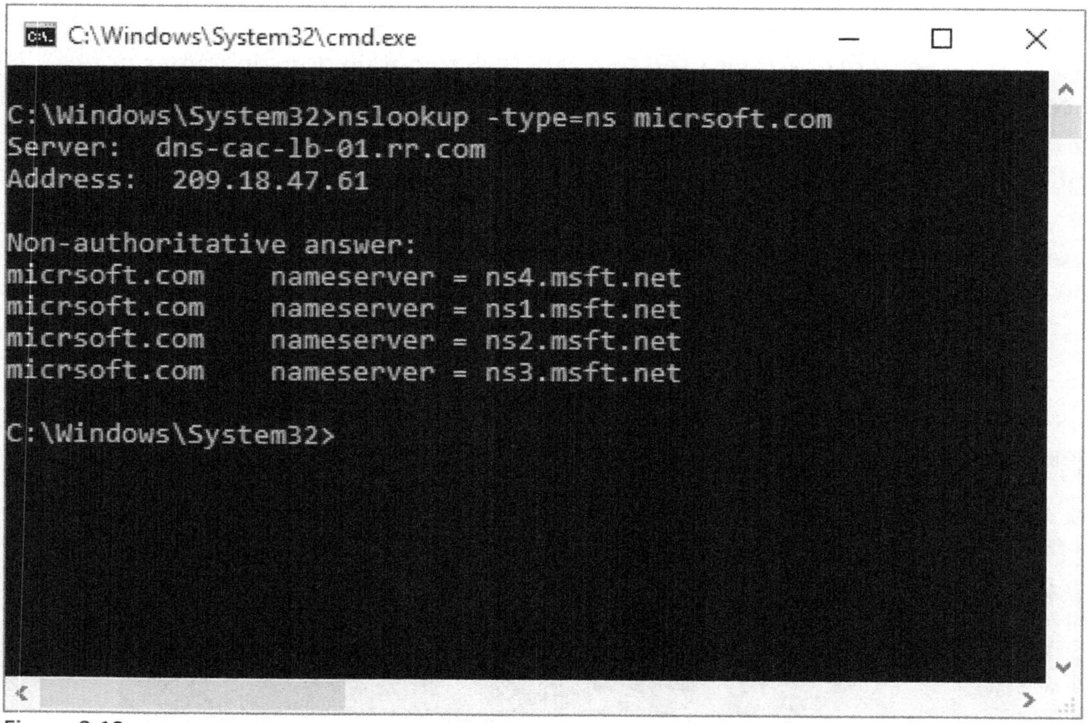

```
C:\Windows\System32\cmd.exe                              —    □    ×

C:\Windows\System32>nslookup -type=ns micrsoft.com
Server:  dns-cac-lb-01.rr.com
Address:  209.18.47.61

Non-authoritative answer:
micrsoft.com       nameserver = ns4.msft.net
micrsoft.com       nameserver = ns1.msft.net
micrsoft.com       nameserver = ns2.msft.net
micrsoft.com       nameserver = ns3.msft.net

C:\Windows\System32>
```

Figure 8.12

If you want to use a different name server to run your queries against instead of your own default server, you can do so with the following command **nslookup domain.com servername.domain.com** or **nslookup domain.com ipaddress** where you are telling the command what you want to look up and the name or IP address of the name server you want to use to do so. So, if we want to lookup microsoft.com using a name server with the IP address of 8.8.8.8 (which is a Google DNS server) we would run the following command:

Nslookup microsoft.com 8.8.8.8

You can see the results in figure 8.13.

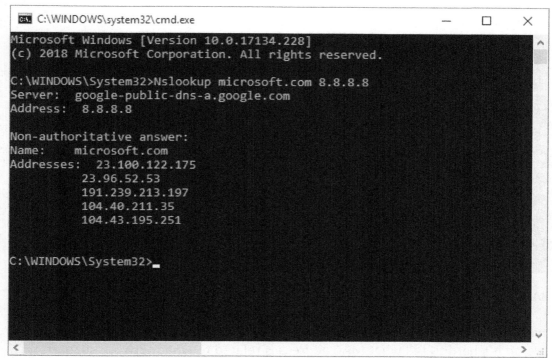

Figure 8.13

You might have noticed that the results mention a *Non-authoritative answer*. What that means is the name server used was not in the list for the domain you did a lookup on. If you see *Authoritative answer* in your results, that means the answer originated from the DNS Server, which has the information about the zone file.

These are not the only things you can do with the nslookup command, so, if you are interested, do a little research on the command and play around with some of the other options.

Getmac

The Getmac command is a simple to use tool that will show you all the MAC addresses and network protocols for the network adapters installed on your computer. If you run the command by itself it will just show you the information for the locally installed adapters that are enabled, as you can see in figure 8.14.

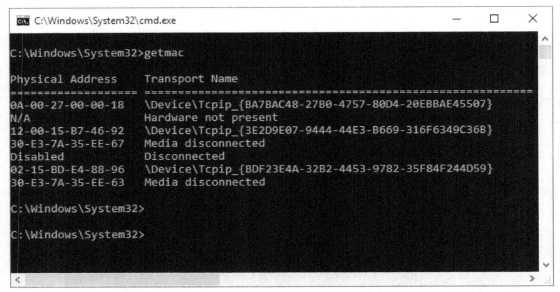

Figure 8.14

One thing you might have noticed is that it doesn't tell you the *names* of the adapters, so it's hard to tell what MAC address is related to what network adapter. If you add **/fo table /nh /v** to the command you get more usable output (figure 8.15)

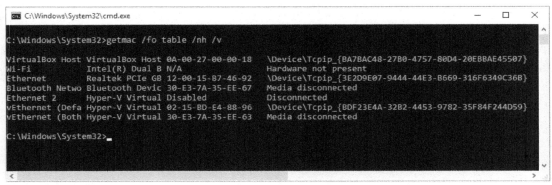

Figure 8.15

- **/fo table** – Specifies the format to use for the query output, with *table* being used in our example.

- **/nh** - Suppresses the column header in the output.

- **/v** – Tells the command to display verbose information.

There are other switches you can use with the Getmac command, and it's also possible to use the command to get information from remote computers.

Nbtstat

This utility is used to show protocol statistics and TCP/IP connections using NetBIOS over TCP/IP, which helps troubleshoot NetBIOS name resolution problems. The NetBIOS name is the name of your computer, such as **computer1**. It's different from a FQDN (Fully Qualified Domain Name) such as **computer1.mydomain.com**.

There are various switches you can use with the Nbtstat command such as **–a**, which will list a remote computer's name table. So, if you type in **nbtstat –a ipaddress** you will get output similar to figure 8.16.

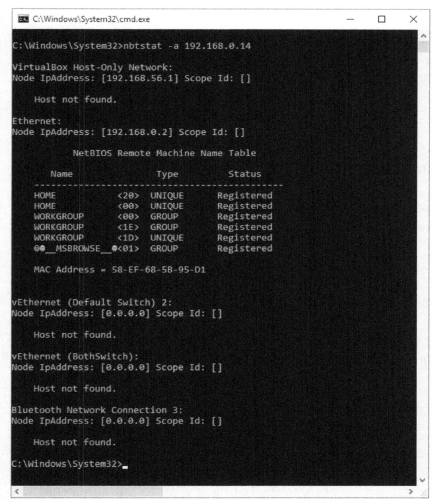

Figure 8.16

As you can see, when we run the command against an IP address of 192.168.0.14 using our Ethernet adapter, we can see the NetBIOS is HOME, the workgroup name is WORKGROUP, and the MAC address is 58-EF-68-5B-95-D1.

Here is a listing of the available switches for the Nbtstat command:

-a   (adapter status) Lists the remote machine's name table given its name.

-A   (Adapter status) Lists the remote machine's name table given its IP address.

-c   (cache) Lists NBT's cache of remote [machine] names and their IP addresses.

-n   (names) Lists local NetBIOS names.

-r   (resolved) Lists names resolved by broadcast and via WINS.

-R   (Reload) Purges and reloads the remote cache name table.

-S   (Sessions) Lists sessions table with the destination IP addresses.

-s   (sessions) Lists sessions table converting destination IP addresses to computer NETBIOS names.

-RR   (ReleaseRefresh) Sends Name Release packets to WINs and then starts Refresh.

RemoteName Remote host machine name.

IP address   Dotted decimal representation of the IP address.

interval   Redisplays selected statistics, pausing interval seconds between each display. Press Ctrl+C to stop redisplaying statistics.

ARP-a

I talked about ARP (Address Resolution Protocol) in Chapter 6 in our discussion of protocols, but there is also an ARP command you can use to display or modify the IP to physical address translation tables used by the ARP protocol. Just like with all the other commands, ARP has its own set of switches, but I just want to talk about the –a switch, which will show the current ARP entries for the cache tables for all your network interfaces. The ARP cache is a basic mapping of IP addresses to MAC addresses. Figure 8.17 shows three different interfaces along with the Internet and physical addresses of hosts that have been resolved via those interfaces. It also shows whether the address type was dynamic or static.

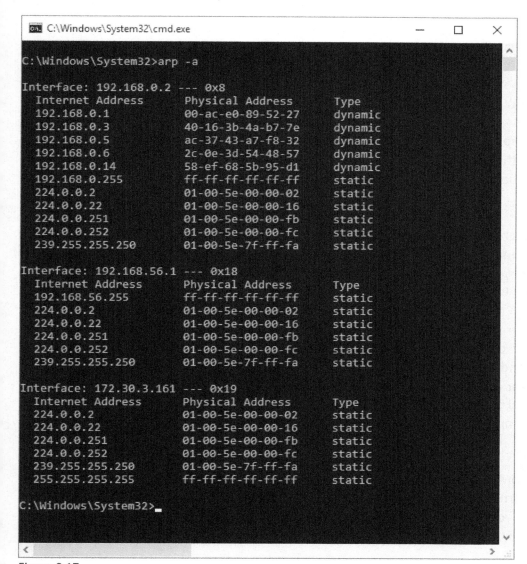

```
C:\Windows\System32\cmd.exe                          —    □    ×

C:\Windows\System32>arp -a

Interface: 192.168.0.2 --- 0x8
  Internet Address      Physical Address      Type
  192.168.0.1           00-ac-e0-89-52-27     dynamic
  192.168.0.3           40-16-3b-4a-b7-7e     dynamic
  192.168.0.5           ac-37-43-a7-f8-32     dynamic
  192.168.0.6           2c-0e-3d-54-48-57     dynamic
  192.168.0.14          58-ef-68-5b-95-d1     dynamic
  192.168.0.255         ff-ff-ff-ff-ff-ff     static
  224.0.0.2             01-00-5e-00-00-02     static
  224.0.0.22            01-00-5e-00-00-16     static
  224.0.0.251           01-00-5e-00-00-fb     static
  224.0.0.252           01-00-5e-00-00-fc     static
  239.255.255.250       01-00-5e-7f-ff-fa     static

Interface: 192.168.56.1 --- 0x18
  Internet Address      Physical Address      Type
  192.168.56.255        ff-ff-ff-ff-ff-ff     static
  224.0.0.2             01-00-5e-00-00-02     static
  224.0.0.22            01-00-5e-00-00-16     static
  224.0.0.251           01-00-5e-00-00-fb     static
  224.0.0.252           01-00-5e-00-00-fc     static
  239.255.255.250       01-00-5e-7f-ff-fa     static

Interface: 172.30.3.161 --- 0x19
  Internet Address      Physical Address      Type
  224.0.0.2             01-00-5e-00-00-02     static
  224.0.0.22            01-00-5e-00-00-16     static
  224.0.0.251           01-00-5e-00-00-fb     static
  224.0.0.252           01-00-5e-00-00-fc     static
  239.255.255.250       01-00-5e-7f-ff-fa     static
  255.255.255.255       ff-ff-ff-ff-ff-ff     static

C:\Windows\System32>_
```

Figure 8.17

You can also run the command against a single IP address by typing in **arp –a 192.168.0.3**, for example, to get the results from just that address.

User Accounts

In order to have a working and secure network you will need user accounts for the people who want to use your networked resources such as computers, file servers, application, printers, and so on.

User configuration is pretty simple do to in Windows, and it's really just a matter of making the user account and giving it the appropriate permissions. The procedure is a little different for workgroup users compared to domain users, but the principals are very similar. For example, you create user accounts on the computer you want the user to be able to access when dealing with workgroups. For domain users, you create the user accounts on domain controllers, which are used to manage all the aspects of a Windows Active Directory Domain.

For workgroup user accounts I had mentioned that there are two basic types you will be using. Rather than make you find that section to review, I will just repeat the information here.

Standard user accounts are for people who need to do everyday tasks on the computer such as run programs, go online, print, and so on. Standard users can also install and uninstall certain software as well. It's usually a good idea to make everyone on your network a standard user, and then if they need something done that requires higher privileges, they can have an administrator do it.

Administrator user accounts have full control over the computer and can do things such as install or uninstall any software, add or remove user accounts, add or remove hardware, and make changes that affect Windows itself. If you are logged in as a standard user and need to do something that requires administrator access, many times you will be prompted to enter the username and password of an administrator so you don't need to actually log out and then back in as an administrator to get the job done.

Like I mentioned, domain or Active Directory user accounts are created on domain controllers from a centralized location. There are many types of user account permissions you can assign to a user. Some examples include account operator, administrator, domain admins, enterprise admins, backup operators, and domain users.

For your standard user accounts you will create them as domain users and then assign them to whatever groups you need them to be a part of for them to be able to do their job. Just like user accounts, there are several built-in groups, including print operators and remote desktop services users. Your regular user accounts are put in the Users group by default, but you can organize them into folders called organizational units (or OUs) like departments and so on. No matter what computer a domain user logs into on the domain, they will get their assigned permissions applied to them on the spot.

Users can be assigned to multiple groups that you can create as needed. When you create these groups, you can assign various levels of permissions to the group, and anyone who is a part of that group will inherit those permissions. Keep in mind that if two groups have permissions that contradict each other, the one with the most restrictive permissions will apply. Groups can be used in workgroups and with domains.

Remote Connections

With everything and everyone being connected these days, telecommuting is becoming more and more common, allowing many of us to work from home as if we were sitting in front of our desk at the office. This can be a good or bad thing depending on how you look at it and how much you are going to abuse your freedom!

Thanks to high speed broadband connections it's easy to have a fast and reliable remote session to the office or any other location with an Internet connection, and there are several ways you can remotely connect to the office, so choosing the right one will make your experience all that much better.

I talked about VPN connections in Chapter 7. These Virtual Private Networks allow us to make a secure connection from one site to another via the Internet, and then we can use this connection for our remote access into the office or other location. Of course, there are other methods that don't require you to make a VPN connection first, but they may not be as secure.

For Windows users one common way to connect to a remote computer over the Internet or even over your network is to use a Remote Desktop connection. Remote Desktop is Microsoft's built-in remote access client that allows you to log into a remote computer and use it as if you were sitting right in front of it.

The Remote Desktop client is built into Windows, and all you need to do to open it is to find it on your Start Menu (most likely under Windows Accessories), or you can do a search for it as well. Another way many people start the program is by typing **mstsc.exe** from the run box.

Once the Remote Desktop client is up and running, you will need to fill in the required information needed to make the connection. All you really need is the IP address or host name of the computer you are going to connect to (figure 8.18). You can also enter the username before logging on or wait for a login prompt to enter the username and password.

Figure 8.18

As you can see in figure 8.18, there are other tabs that you can use to configure the Remote Desktop settings before you make the connection.

- **General** – Here you will enter the computer's hostname or IP address that you want to connect to, as well as the username if you like.

- **Display** – This is where you can set a custom screen resolution and color quality.

- **Local Resources** – If you want things like sounds from the remote computer or access to the remote computer's printer and Windows clipboard, you can enable these things here.

- **Experience** – In this section you can alter the quality of your session based on various connection speeds.

- **Advanced** – Here you can change the security settings for server authentication as well as the Remote Desktop Gateway settings.

You might have noticed on the General tab that there were options to save the connection settings. This comes in handy if it's a connection that you use all the time and you just want an icon on your desktop that you can double click to open the connection each time.

 It's generally not a good idea to save credentials for any computer you access, especially if you have administrator rights on that computer. That would be the same as removing the password from your desktop and allowing anyone who walks by access to it.

Once you make the connection, it will look just like you are sitting at the remote computer and all of the Windows settings such as desktop icons and mapped drives etc. will all be in place for you. If you want to switch back and forth between your local computer and the remote computer all you need to do is minimize the Remote Desktop window.

One other remote connection type I want to talk about is the type that is hosted by a third party server such as TeamViewer or LogMeIn. When using these type of remote access methods you are not using a VPN client on your computer or changing firewall configuration settings to make the connection, but rather you use either a web browser plugin or some type of locally installed application that facilitates the connection. This connection takes place on the company's server, usually through port 80, so there won't be any firewall issues since port 80 is also used for website traffic.

The way these connections are secured are by using a unique code and password for the session, and the computer that will be controlled needs to provide these credentials to initiate the connection. Once the party on either end closes the session, then it will have to be reinitiated. Some of these products will allow you to leave them running so you can connect without someone being on the other end, but that might not be the most secure thing to do.

Chapter 9 – Virtualization & Cloud Computing

Today's modern datacenter is much different than it was 5-10 years ago, and is still evolving and changing at a rapid pace. With technology advancing so quickly, the days of the datacenter full of big clunky servers are over. Nowadays everything is being virtualized or run from "the cloud", allowing us to do more with less hardware.

Virtualization
Many modern datacenters are turning to a technology known as virtualization to downsize on the amount of physical servers that take up space, power, and financial resources. These physical servers are replaced with virtual servers that run within virtualization software installed on a physical server.

With virtualization technology, those same physical servers can run multiple virtual servers (VMs) on just one piece of hardware, and each VM can have its own operating system, hard drives, CPU, memory, and so on. Of course, to be able to pull this off, the actual physical server needs to have enough physical resources available to run the amount of virtual servers you want to host on that physical server. You are limited by your hardware resources when it comes to the amount of virtual servers and their "virtual" hardware specs.

In order to utilize virtualization technology, you need software that will allow you to virtualize servers so that they can run with other servers on the same piece of hardware (physical server) and access the physical devices on that piece of hardware. There are a several vendors out there that offer this type of software, and I will get to this next.

To make this all work, the hardware manufacturers (specifically processor manufacturers) need to have the CPUs be able to support multiple servers with multiple operating systems at the same time. The physical server is typically called the *host*, while the virtual servers (or VMs) are called *guests*. The software used to make this all happen is called a hypervisor, and this hypervisor interacts with the physical hardware and allows the hardware to be used by the VMs. The hypervisor also monitors the physical hardware and allows you to see what is going on with the assigned resources being used by the VMs.

Figure 9.1 shows a physical server with a hypervisor running on top of it. Then that hypervisor allow you to create your virtual machines, install an operating system on them, and then install applications within that operating system. Then you have the storage physically attached to the server, and the hypervisor then uses that storage to allocate disk space to the VMs.

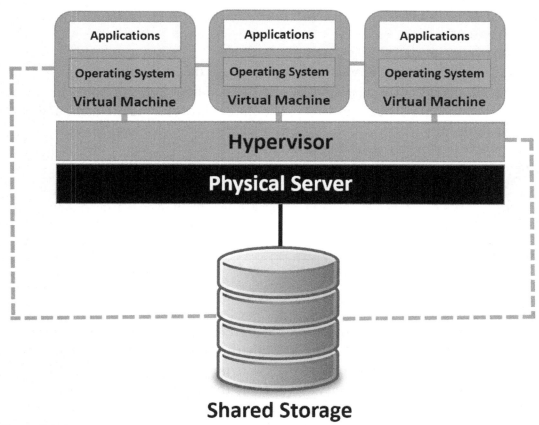

Figure 9.1

The management software is what the administrator uses to manage all the VMs and their virtual devices and storage. It also allows you to create new VMs and move them from host to host while they are running, allowing you to do things such as perform maintenance on the host or balance the load. Other things you do with this software is configure the virtual switches and virtual network cards for your network configuration, add storage to VMs, create clusters for resource allocation, check errors and alerts, manage licensing, and much more.

If you have physical servers that you want to virtualize without having to create them from scratch, you can perform a P2V (Physical to Virtual) with separate software and convert the physical server to a virtual machine with its operating system and applications intact. This can be a time consuming procedure with limitations, but usually works out pretty well.

All in all virtualization is a great technology that gives you a number of benefits, including:

- Saving money on hardware and maintenance costs;
- Freeing up rack space;
- More uptime;
- Keep your server room cooler;
- Allows easier backup of servers with built-in or third party software;
- Save on Windows licensing (depending on the number of VMs on a host);
- Allows you to move virtualized servers to different hosts for maintenance and host failures.

If you plan on making a career out of working on computers and networks, then you are going to need to get some experience with virtualization platforms, since most companies are virtualized these days.

Virtualization Software

As I mentioned earlier, in order to implement virtual machines in a virtualized environment you will need to install some sort of virtualization platform onto your physical server to run the virtual machines in. This hypervisor, as it's called, can be installed on supported physical servers, and then all these physical servers can be monitored from one management console. The management console can also monitor your VMs as well as your virtual infrastructure. There are several vendors that offer this type of platform that you can use in your environment. I will now discuss two of the biggest players in the game.

VMware

VMware has their flagship product called vSphere, and it's their enterprise level hypervisor capable of supporting thousands of VMs at multiple sites. You can run a variety of operating systems on their platform (including Windows, Linux, and Apple OS X) and used shared storage and networking resources to design the configuration you need for your business.

Their hypervisor is named ESXi and their management platform is called vCenter, and it's a web based management console that allows you to configure VMs, hosts, storage, networking, and other components. VMware also has other products to complement their vSphere product, such as cloud offerings and virtual desktops for end users.

Hyper-V

Microsoft has their own virtualization platform called Hyper-V, which runs on top of the Windows operating system. Hyper-V was first available with Windows Server 2008, and is still included with all the Windows Server releases. If you have Windows 8 or Windows 10, you can run a scaled down version of Hyper-V on your desktop (figure 9.1). The only requirement is that your version of Windows must be a 64 bit edition running Professional, Enterprise, or Education.

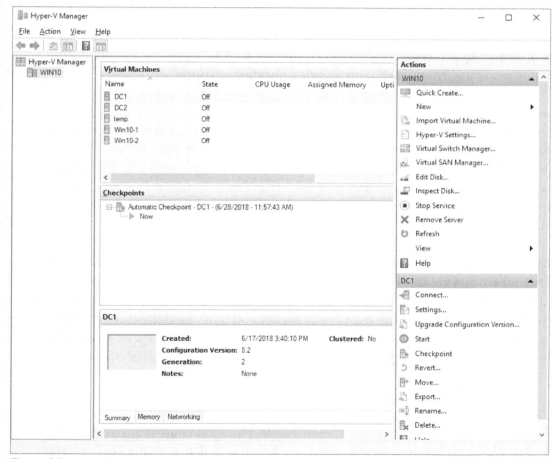

Figure 9.2

Only Windows guest operating systems are supported on Hyper-V, but you can still run Linux with some limitations and lack of support. And since Hyper-V is included With Windows, all you need to do is enable the feature and you are ready to go (assuming you have the horsepower in your server to run multiple VMs and the storage available to assign to those VMs). Keep in mind that you need to pay for the Windows license, so it's not a totally free feature.

VirtualBox

I did want to mention one more virtualization product before we move on. If you want to play around with creating VMs at home and don't have the money to buy a VMware license or a Windows server license and don't have the right version of Windows 8 or 10, then a great solution to that problem is to use Oracle's VirtualBox virtualization software. It's free to use and fairly easy to understand and configure, and you will have your own virtual machines up and running in no time.

VirtualBox supports Windows, Linux, and Mac OS X guest operating systems, and you can use your locally attached hard drives as storage for those guests. You can install it on Windows, Linux, Macintosh, and Solaris operating systems.

Storage

In order to create VMs and assign them disk space for things like the operating system, you need some type of storage that you can allocate to the VMs themselves. Configuring storage for the hosts and guests is typically done with shared storage such as a SAN (Storage Area Network) or NAS (Network Attached Storage) for the guests, and local storage for the hosts in the form of a hard drive, USB drive, or SD card, but the host can also be configured to use shared storage.

The storage is usually a group of disk arrays separate from the hosts that are attached to the hosts via iSCSI or Fiber Channel. This networked storage is configured with LUNs (Logical Unit Numbers), which are like volumes configured for use within the virtualized environment. The hypervisor allows you to make datastores with this storage, and then these datastores can be used for the guest VMs as their local storage to install the operating system as well as be used for additional drives.

Cloud Services

Another trend that has been taking off over the last several years is the concept of using cloud services for some or all of your IT infrastructure. This way all the hardware and configurations are stored at the cloud service provider's location and you access the things you need (such as file services or email servers) over the Internet rather than on your own local network.

By doing this companies can utilize resources as they need them rather than buying a bunch of hardware to install locally for huge amounts of money. Of course, with cloud services you are paying a monthly fee, but you also don't have to worry about being responsible for the infrastructure in case something breaks unless it's something tied to what you are using the resources for (such as your domain controller having a configuration issue).

There are various services you can use in the cloud, and they all have some fancy names such as Software as a Service (SaaS), Platform as a Service (PaaS), Infrastructure as a Service (IaaS), and Network as a Service (NaaS). Which service or services you decide to use will determine what you can do with these services.

- **SaaS** – This is the simplest type of cloud service because you only have control over the software that you are using and not things like the servers, network, storage, and so on. An example of SaaS would be Google Docs.

- **PaaS** – This is where you are given a platform to run your software on. You are not responsible for things like operating system maintenance, but you do have control over things like the servers, networking, and storage. An example of PaaS would be Microsoft Azure.

- **IaaS** – This cloud service level provides you with the most control over the resources that you are paying to use. You control the VMs, networking, storage, and so on, giving you the freedom to configure things the way you like while the service provider simply provides you with the means to do so. An example of IaaS would be Amazon Web Services.

- **NaaS** – NaaS is used when companies don't want to build their own network infrastructure on site and rely on the service provider to provide them with everything they need to get their network built and operational. This can reduce costs as well as the amount of time needed for your IT staff to maintain the network.

Like I mentioned above, Microsoft Azure and Amazon Web Services (AWS) are two of the biggest cloud service providers in the game today. You can run your whole business in the cloud using their infrastructure (assuming you have the money to pay for it!). Both of them offer free trials, so if you want to get a taste of how cloud services work, you should check them out. Just be careful and watch your utilization because they will want to charge you once you go over your free limits, which really aren't much to begin with.

Home User Could Services
If you want to get a taste of how basic cloud services work, then you can get yourself a free cloud storage account. For most of them you can access your files via their website and also have a client on your computer that will sync your local files with your files in the cloud if that is what you are looking to do. There are many companies that provide high level cloud storage with all sorts of options as to storage capacity and performance, but for the average home user or small business owner, you can stick with one of the "name brand" cloud providers and be just fine. Here is a list of the most commonly use ones:

- **DropBox** – DropBox has been around for years, and is probably the most commonly used basic cloud provider service. They will give you 2-5GB of free storage (depending on your plan), and then after that you will need to pay for an upgrade. The cost will vary depending on how much storage you need. The cheapest 1TB plan starts at $9.99\month.

- **Microsoft OneDrive** – Microsoft has gotten into the cloud storage game with its OneDrive software, which always seems to end up on your computer whether you asked for it or not. They have a 5GB free plan, and then they go up from there with the next level costing $1.99\month for 50GB. They have some pricier options that Include an Office 365 software subscription.

- **Google Drive** – Google offers you 15GB of free storage, and for $1.99\month you can upgrade to 100GB. The capacity and storage amounts go up from there.

- **Amazon Drive** – Amazon gives you 5GB of storage for free just for being an Amazon customer. If you are an Amazon Prime member, you get unlimited photo storage. For $11.99\year you can get 100GB of storage.

- **iCloud Storage** – Apple has their own cloud storage for all of your Apple devices such as your Mac, iPhone, and iPad, and you will get 5GB for free automatically. If you need additional storage, you can pay for it just like with the other cloud storage providers. For example, a 50GB plan will cost you $0.99 a month.

Other free cloud services you can try out include things like Google Docs and Microsoft Office Online, which is a free version of their Office 365 package, but doesn't include all the features. The main programs included with Office Online include Word, Excel, PowerPoint, and OneNote, but there are other apps you can use with Office Online, such as Mail, Calendar, and OneDrive. Your files will be saved to your OneDrive location by default, but you do have the option to download them to your local computer. To use Office Online all you need to do is sign in with your Microsoft account or create one if you don't have one. For Google Docs you just need a Gmail account and you can use their versions of Office-like programs.

Chapter 10 – Network Troubleshooting

Now that you have your network up and running and things are looking good, what do you do when something breaks and your computers are not communicating with each other anymore? That's when you need to put on your troubleshooting hat and get down to business. But where do you start? In this chapter I am going to go over some basic troubleshooting steps you can take to see if you can get your network talking again.

Hardware Issues
First I would like to talk about potential hardware issues you can face with your networking equipment. Trying to figuring out hardware issues is the first step in determining what exactly is being affected by the current problem. Is it just one computer? Is your Internet access down? Or is it a group of devices that can't connect?

If it's just one computer that is down then I would first check the network connection status from the operating system itself. With Windows it's pretty simple because you will have a network connection status icon in the system tray down by the clock. If it has a yellow exclamation point or red X through it, then you know there is a network problem that is affecting Windows.

On the back of the computer where the Ethernet cable is plugged in you can check to see if there is a green link light indicating a connection to the device on the other end of the cable. If the light is amber\orange that usually means it's running at a slower speed (such as 100Mbps), or it can sometimes mean there is a problem. There is no real standard to what color means what, so you are kind of stuck guessing. Some network cards even have two lights, one for the link connection and one that flashes for activity. If there is no light, then there is definitely a problem with either the network card, the cable, or maybe the device it's connected to on the other end.

To see if Windows is having a problem with your network card you should check Device Manager because it may help to give you an idea as to why it's not working. If you don't see your network card in the list of hardware under *network adapters,* then that means Windows does not recognize it and it could be dead. You may also have a problem with a driver or conflict with another device. If that's the case, you may see a yellow question mark or exclamation point next to the device.

The easiest way to get to Device Manager is just to do a search for it from the run box at the Start menu. Then you will see a list similar to figure 10.1, but you most likely won't have as many items under network adapters unless you are using some sort of virtualization software like I discussed in the last chapter.

Figure 10.1

As you can see there is an issue with the device called Hyper-V Virtual Switch Extension Adapter #2. Right clicking the device will give you options to do things like update the driver or disable the device, as well as view its properties. As you can see in figure 10.2, the General tab of the device's properties shows that there is a code 10 error saying the device cannot start. You can use this information to start your researching to find out what the cause might be.

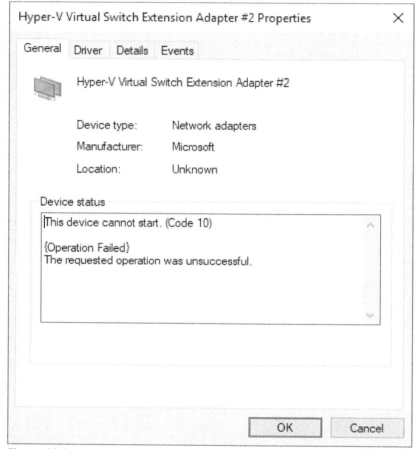

Figure 10.2

You may also want to try and download and install a newer drive for the device that is having the problem. Sometimes even uninstalling the device and rebooting the computer to make it reinstall the device will give it the kick it needs to start working again, so it's worth a shot.

So let's say your computer is working fine and there are no errors in Device Manager or in the device settings of whatever operating system you are using. You can then look at what device your computer is connected to. If you are connected to a network switch, you can try another free port on the switch and see if your connection comes back. This is assuming that the other port you tried is configured the same and is not on something like a different VLAN. If you have another computer that is working fine that you can disconnect from the network, then you can try and use its switch port to see if your connectivity comes back. If multiple computers that are connected to the same switch are not working, then you can assume you are having a switch problem. You might get lucky and fix it with a simple switch reboot, but keep in mind that any devices that are working on that switch will go down.

If your problem only involves no Internet connection but the network is working fine, then you should look at your modem or whatever device provides your Internet connection. Check all the status lights on the modem and make sure nothing is out that shouldn't be and nothing is flashing that shouldn't be. Even if everything looks to be in order, you can try to reboot the modem to reset it and have it try and reconnect and get its settings again. Also be sure to check the link light on the back of the modem and the switch port it plugs into.

Cabling Issues
I'm sure you were wondering why I didn't mention checking the cables when discussing the possible hardware issues and checking link lights etc. That's because I wanted to do a separate section just on cabling issues.

Ethernet Cables
Network cables don't last forever, and they can get damaged from things such as rolling your chair over them and bending them too much or too far. The ends can also get damaged to where the wires inside the RJ45 plus lose their connection from things like tugging too hard on them.

If you are having a connection problem and everything on the computer looks okay hardware wise and switching ports on the switch or router doesn't make a difference, then you should try to replace the cable (assuming it's something you are able to access).

If it's a jack in the wall with the cabling going inside the wall and through the ceiling, then you will not be able to replace the cable to test. Or at least it won't be an easy task. In that case you can use a cable tester\toner to see if the connection from the wall jack to wherever it terminates is good (figure 10.3). One end plugs into the Ethernet port and then you take the toner wand on the other end to see if there is a proper signal going through the wire. If you don't get a tone then there is a broken connection somewhere in the cable, and that's where the fun part begins because you will need to track it down. You can also use these testers to test cables that you make yourself before putting them in production.

Figure 10.3

Another potential problem with cabling is if it has been run by something that is giving off electrical interference, which can be radio frequency interference (RFI) or electromagnetic interference (EMI). These can occur when things like radio frequency energy causes an electrical device to produce noise that can interfere with the function of an adjacent device. You can have cases of RFI or EMI when you run your cables too close to things like power relays, cordless phones, microwaves, air conditioning units, lights, and so on. If this is the cause of your problem, then you can either reroute your network cable, remove the object causing the interference, or switch to STP cable (Shielded Twisted Pair). STP is a standard Ethernet cable, but each pair of wires are covered by an additional copper braid jacket or foil wrapping (figure 10.4).

Figure 10.4

Like I mentioned before, you should also look for crimps in the cable or see if someone moved a desk on top of the cable and so on. The wires inside an Ethernet cable are pretty flexible, but if you bend them over and over enough times they will eventually break apart. The RJ45 connectors are also crimped onto the cable, so make sure nothing got pulled apart and that all the wires inside the connector are making contact. The ends are usually clear, and if you have good eyes you can usually see if one or more of the connections are not being made. If that's the case, you will either need to replace the cable or redo the RJ45 connector on the end of the cable by cutting off the old one and crimping on a new one.

One last thing I want to mention about Ethernet cables is that you can only go about 100 meters (or about 328 feet) with your cable run before you need to regenerate the signal, otherwise you will suffer from what they call signal attenuation, which is when the signal strength gradually decreases over the length of the cable until it's not strong enough to pass the data. In order to get around this 100 meter limit you will need to "repeat" the signal to regenerate it. This can be done by running it through a switch or hub, and that will give you another 100 meters until it needs to be repeated again.

Fiber Optic Cables
Although fiber optic cables don't have the same problems as Ethernet cables, that doesn't mean they are perfect. These cables can get damaged or fail for other reasons as well. As you can see in figure 10.5, a fiber optic cable is made up of several components, including an outer jacket, plastic buffer, glass cladding, and a glass core to carry the signal (although it can also be plastic).

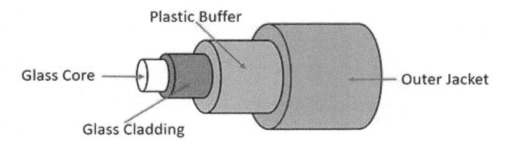

Figure 10.5

Fiber optic cables are a little more delicate that Ethernet cables due to their glass components, so you can't bend them as much and they can still be damaged by placing objects on top of them. On the other hand, they don't suffer from the same RFI\EMI interference as Ethernet cables do.

There is still a limit on how far you can run a fiber optic cable before the signal needs to be regenerated though. It's a much greater distance than Ethernet and varies based on the type of cable you are using, but just like with Ethernet, if you have a faulty connector or splice in the cable, then you are looking at replacing that cable or at least the connector (which is not an easy job to do and takes a specialist). Another possible issue that can cause connection problems is a lack of transmitting power from the device sending the signal. Just like with Ethernet, there are fiber optic cable testers as well (figure 10.6), but they are a little more expensive depending on what features you want.

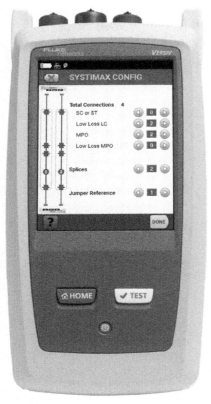

Figure 10.6

As you can see, there are many ways a cable can be the cause of your network issue, so it's important to know what to look for when diagnosing a potential cable issue.

Wireless Issues

You might think that having no network cables would make things work more smoothly, but if you were thinking that then you would be wrong! Wireless technology is spreading to almost every device you can think of, but it still comes with its own set of problems. The first step in troubleshooting wireless connections is to see if your computer is connected to your wireless router\access point. The first place you should look is at your wireless connection, and the easiest way to do that for Windows users is to click on your wireless connection icon in your system tray down by the clock (as shown in figure 10.6). This will tell you if your computer is connected to your access point, and if not, then the first thing you need to do is reconnect it. If it doesn't want to connect, then there is an issue with your access point or the wireless device on your computer. You can try to reboot\reset your access point and see if that fixes it, or try to connect to your access point with a

127

different device such as your smartphone or tablet. If other devices connect successfully, then you know it's the computer that has the problem.

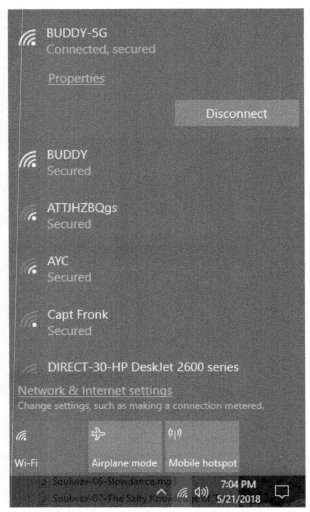

Figure 10.6

Another place you can look to see connectivity status is the Network and Sharing Center in Control Panel (figure 10.7). Here you will be able to see what network your computer is connected to and the connection name. Next to where it says *Access type*, it will say if your computer has Internet access or not.

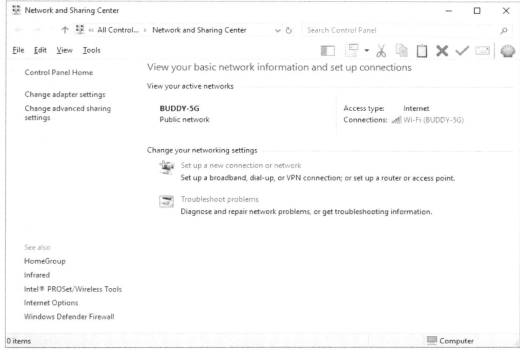

Figure 10.7

If you click on the name of the connection you will get details such as the SSID (service set identifier), which is the name of the wireless access point you are connecting to, the connection speed, and also the signal quality if it's a wireless connection (figure 10.8).

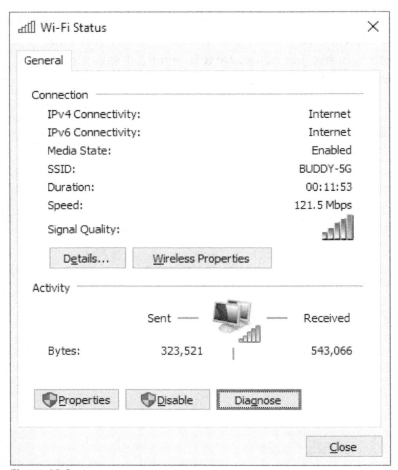

Figure 10.8

Clicking on the Details button will tell you more advanced information about the connection, such as the IP address, subnet mask, default gateway, DHCP server, and DNS server (figure 10.9). If you don't have anything shown for these settings, then that is most likely your problem.

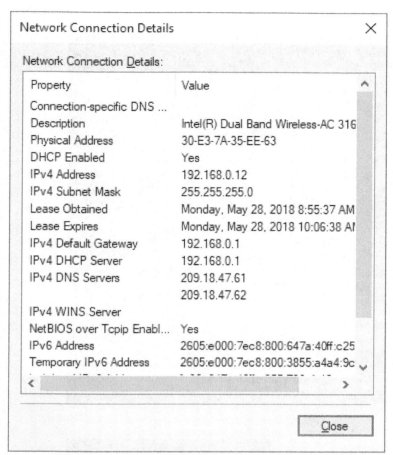

Figure 10.9

Clicking the Diagnose button, as seen in figure 10.8, will start the Windows Network Diagnostics, which may be able to determine why you can't get on the Internet and fix the problem for you. Sometimes this utility works great, and sometimes it's a waste of time, but it's worth trying out.

If your connection to your access point is working, then you will want to see if your computer has an IP address, subnet mask, and default gateway. All of these are needed to make a successful connection to the Internet or any other type of network. You can check this information from the details area as shown in figure 10.9, or from a command prompt. Open a command prompt by typing **cmd** from the run box or Cortana search box and then type **ipconfig**. Then press enter, and it will show you similar information (figure 10.10).

```
Select C:\WINDOWS\system32\cmd.exe                                 —   □   ✕
(c) 2017 Microsoft Corporation. All rights reserved.

C:\WINDOWS\System32>ipconfig

Windows IP Configuration


Ethernet adapter Ethernet:

   Media State . . . . . . . . . . . : Media disconnected
   Connection-specific DNS Suffix  . :

Ethernet adapter VirtualBox Host-Only Network:

   Connection-specific DNS Suffix  . :
   Link-local IPv6 Address . . . . . : fe80::ac7e:bee0:8d26:a46d%15
   IPv4 Address. . . . . . . . . . . : 192.168.56.1
   Subnet Mask . . . . . . . . . . . : 255.255.255.0
   Default Gateway . . . . . . . . . :

Wireless LAN adapter Local Area Connection* 3:

   Media State . . . . . . . . . . . : Media disconnected
   Connection-specific DNS Suffix  . :

Wireless LAN adapter Wi-Fi:

   Connection-specific DNS Suffix  . :
   IPv6 Address. . . . . . . . . . . : 2605:e000:7ec8:800:647a:40ff:c255:736a
   Temporary IPv6 Address. . . . . . : 2605:e000:7ec8:800:3855:a4a4:9c28:d591
   Link-local IPv6 Address . . . . . : fe80::647a:40ff:c255:736a%12
   IPv4 Address. . . . . . . . . . . : 192.168.0.12
   Subnet Mask . . . . . . . . . . . : 255.255.255.0
   Default Gateway . . . . . . . . . : fe80::2ac:e0ff:fe89:5227%12
                                       192.168.0.1
```

Figure 10.10

If you *do* have an IP address and its starts with 169.254, then that is called an APIPA (Automatic Private IP Addressing) address, which I mentioned in Chapter 4. But to review, this type of IP address is assigned to a computer that has DHCP enabled, but *can't* get a valid IP address from a DHCP server. In most cases the modem or router acts as the DHCP server and gives out IP addresses to the computers and other devices that try to connect to it for Internet access. So, if you see an APIPA address, then you need to look into your modem, router, or whatever device your computer is supposed to get its IP address from, because you can only use an APIPA IP address to communicate with other devices using APIPA IP addresses.

If all of your hardware appears to be functioning properly and you have a valid IP address, then there are some other troubleshooting steps you can perform on your computer. Many times a software or spyware issue can prevent your web browser from accessing web pages properly, so it will look as though your Internet connection is not working when it's really just a browser problem. One simple test you can run is to ping a website to see if it makes the connection (Ping was discussed in Chapter 8).

To ping a website, open a command prompt and type in **ping** followed by the website name or IP address and press enter. As you can see in figure 10.11, we ran the command against the website called oninecomputertips.com and got four replies back. Also notice the time of the replies ranging from 28ms (milliseconds) to 61ms. If you get some really large numbers or big discrepancies in times between the four replies, that can indicate a performance issue.

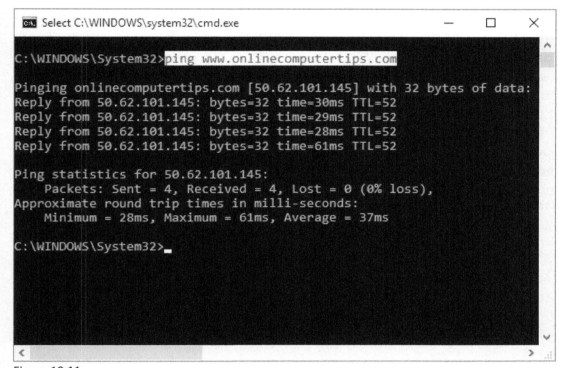

Figure 10.11

Some websites don't allow themselves to be pinged, so if you try one and it fails then try another one before assuming the problem is on your end.

Another test you can run is to see if your email client is working for sending and receiving emails. If so, then that proves you have an Internet connection and that there is just something wrong with your web browser. This only applies to locally installed email clients and not for webmail accounts, since they are accessed via web pages.

If you have more than one web browser, then you should try and use a different one to see if that allows you to access the Internet. If so, then you know the problem lies within your other web browser and may be a case of a configuration change or spyware infection that has altered its settings. If you only have one web browser, you can try to download another one from a different computer, put it on a flash drive, and then install it on your computer and test it out to see if it works.

One other thing you can do is look at the Windows hosts file on your computer. This file is used to map IP addresses to computer or host names and is not really used these days, but still exists within Windows. Many virus and spyware infections will edit this file to redirect your computer to malicious sites or block other sites that can be used to download tools to remove these infections, so it's a good idea to take a look at this file.

To open the hosts file use Windows\File Explorer and browse to **C:\Windows\System32\drivers\etc**. Double click on the file named *hosts*. It will ask what program you want to use to open it, so just use Notepad. As you can see in figure 10.12, it's a pretty simple file with a description of what it is used for and some examples.

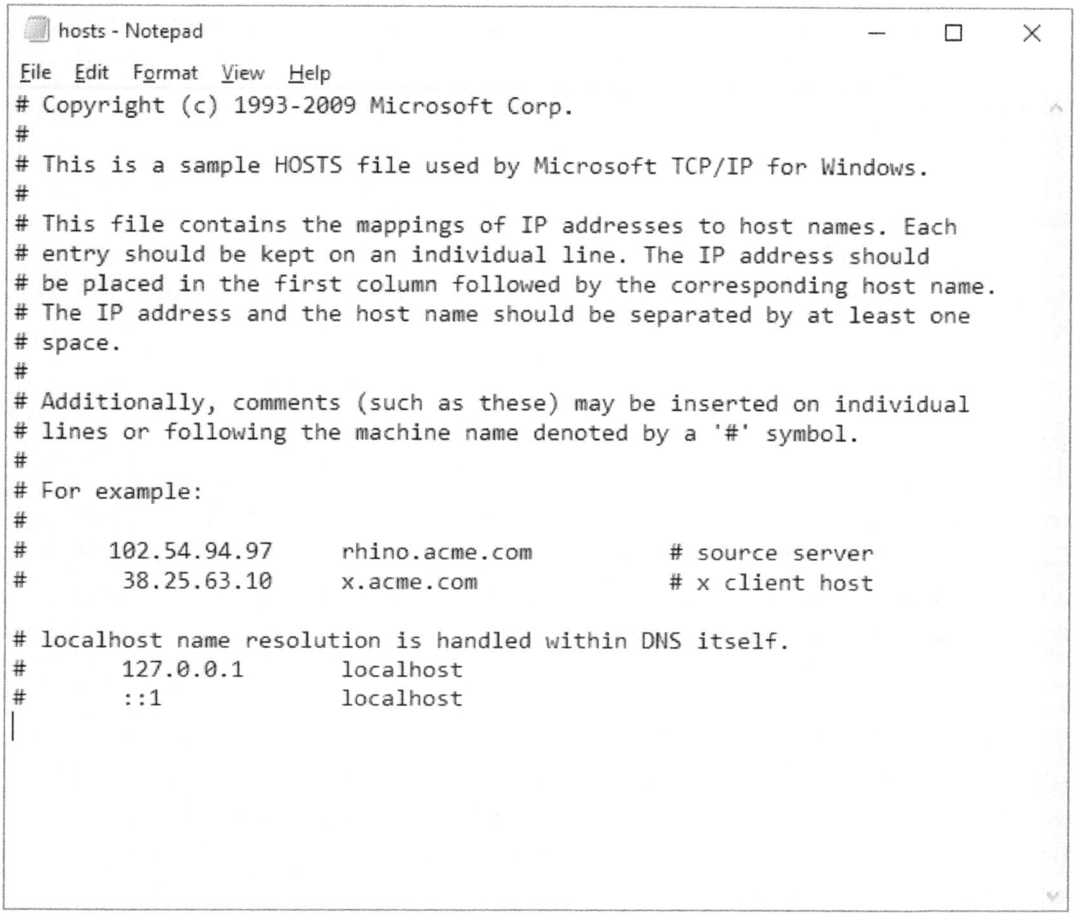

```
hosts - Notepad                                    —    □    ✕

File  Edit  Format  View  Help
# Copyright (c) 1993-2009 Microsoft Corp.
#
# This is a sample HOSTS file used by Microsoft TCP/IP for Windows.
#
# This file contains the mappings of IP addresses to host names. Each
# entry should be kept on an individual line. The IP address should
# be placed in the first column followed by the corresponding host name.
# The IP address and the host name should be separated by at least one
# space.
#
# Additionally, comments (such as these) may be inserted on individual
# lines or following the machine name denoted by a '#' symbol.
#
# For example:
#
#      102.54.94.97     rhino.acme.com          # source server
#       38.25.63.10     x.acme.com              # x client host

# localhost name resolution is handled within DNS itself.
#      127.0.0.1        localhost
#       ::1             localhost
```

Figure 10.12

Any line with # in front of it is just read as text by Windows and will not affect the host file configuration. For the most part, you shouldn't have anything listed here that doesn't have a # in front of it, otherwise that might indicate a problem. It may or may not be obvious if there is something in the file that should not be, so be careful when making any changes unless you are sure of what you are doing. Also, be sure to run a virus and spyware scan afterwards to clean up any infections you might have on your computer that could be affecting your Internet connectivity.

If none of these methods work and you have narrowed down the problem to your computer and not your modem, router, or other network device, then you could be looking at a Windows networking issue, which will involve some further research, but there are other steps you can use to try and narrow it down such as resetting the Windows TCP/IP stack.

Software Issues

Networking is not just about hardware such as switches and routers. There is a lot of software involved to get devices talking to each other over the network. I discussed things like protocols and ports earlier in this book, so now I want to go over some of the more useful ones that you can use to check your software settings and configuration that might help get you out of a bind.

Utilities

Back in Chapter 8 I mentioned a bunch of network utilities you can use to troubleshoot network connectivity problems, so I figured I would mention some of them again here to help you use the right tool for the job. Since these tools are meant to diagnose software related issues, they can be used after you have concluded that your problem is not hardware related.

- **Ping** – Use ping to test simple connectivity between two networked devices. From a command prompt type in **ping** then the IP address and press enter. An example would be **ping 192.168.1.25**. Then wait to see if you get a reply from the other end or if you get a time out or other error such as TTL expired in transit, destination host unreachable, request timed out, or unknown host. Ping might not work if it's being blocked by a firewall etc. on the device you are trying to ping.

- **Tracert** – Use this to trace the route from one device to another to see if something along the path is failing. It will show you each hop on the way to the destination, so you can see where the connection fails. An example would be **tracert 192.168.1.25**. Just remember that the command is actually **traceroute** for Linux and Mac.

- **Pathping** – Pathping is a combination of ping and tracert, so if you want the best of both worlds give this a shot. An example would be **pathping 192.168.1.25**.

- **NSlookup** – If you are having DNS name resolution problems (such as you can only connect to another computer by its IP address and not by its name), then you can use NSlookup to test your DNS settings. Just be sure to use the **ipconfig /all** command first to see what your computer is using for its DNS servers, because that is what the command will use for its lookup unless you tell it to use another DNS server. If your computer is set to use a public\external DNS server like the one provided with your ISP, then you won't be able resolve internal hostnames using that server because it doesn't know anything about your internal network. In many office settings they use an internal DNS server as well to resolve local hostnames.

- **IPconfig** – This command is very useful to check the IP configuration settings on a computer to see if the network communication issue is on your computer rather than on the network. From here you can make sure you have an IP address that is on the right network and that the subnet mask and default gateway are correct as well. If you are using DHCP to get your IP address, you can make sure the right DHCP server is listed as well. If you are having name resolution problems, you can check which DNS servers you are using from here. Just make sure to use the **/all** switch when running the command, and don't forget that for Linux the command is **ifconfig**.

Wireshark

There are many third party utilities out there that can help you diagnose network problems, but there is one that I want to mention because it stands out above the rest and has been the go-to software for network administrators for many years and can provide you will all kinds of information about your network.

The software I am referring to is called Wireshark. It's free to use, but at the same time it's not the type of software that you can just install and use without learning how to use it first. Wireshark is what they call a network protocol analyzer, and can perform live captures of your network traffic so you can analyze it afterwards. You can even save your captures and send them off to others to analyze. It also has a LAN\WAN analyzer and can do VoIP (Voice over IP) analysis. Wireshark can also run on Windows, Linux, UNIX, and Mac OS.

Once you get Wireshark up and running, you can start capturing packets on your network so that you can run you analysis on that data and examine its contents. With this data you can troubleshoot network problems, investigate security issues, test network applications, debug protocol implementations, and so on.

In figure 10.13 I used Wireshark to open a sample capture file, and you can see how the interface is structured. In the top section (called the "packet list pane") is the source and destination IP addresses of each packet and protocol used along with some potentially helpful information next to each entry. The middle pane is called the "packet details" pane, and it shows the protocols and protocol fields of the packet selected from the packet list pane. As you click an item from the first pane, the contents of the second pane will change accordingly. Finally, the last area is called the "packet bytes" pane, and is a canonical hex dump of the packet data.

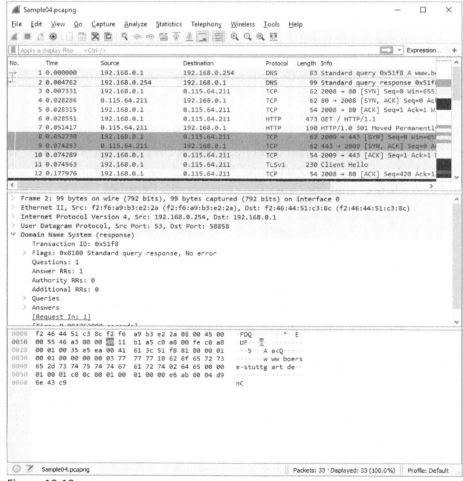

Figure 10.13

Like I mentioned, Wireshark is not a tool for beginners because if you don't know how to read the data in the capture, then it will not be of much use to you. They offer training courses and videos you can watch to learn how to use it, and when you do, you will impress all of your coworkers for sure!

What's Next

Now that you have read through this book, you've hopefully learned a few things and are not more confused about networking than when you started the book! Once you have the basic foundation of how networks function down, then you can start getting into the more advanced stuff and it will make more sense. But if you don't have the basics down, then you will most likely struggle with the higher level stuff.

I would re-read sections that were a little harder to comprehend and then make notes of what information you would like explained a little better. Then you can go and do some research on your own or find some training videos to help you better understand the information. Believe it or not, YouTube has some great videos (and not so great videos) on all kinds of computer related topics. Pluralsight.com is also a great subscription-based video training site, and they have videos on everything you can imagine.

If you want to go the certification route, I would start with the CompTIA Network+ certification, and then you can work your way to the Cisco stuff. The entry level Cisco certification is called the CCENT which stands for Cisco Certified Entry Networking Technician. There are two CCENT certifications, and if you pass both, then you automatically become a CCNA or Cisco Certified Network Associate, which is the next level up. You can also take the CCNA test without the CCENT tests if you feel you know your stuff!

Thanks for reading *Networking Made Easy: Get Yourself Connected*. You can also check out the other books in the *Made Easy* series for additional computer related information and training.

You should also check out our website at www.onlinecomputertips.com, as well as follow us on Facebook at https://www.facebook.com/OnlineComputerTips/ to find more information on all kinds of computer topics.

About the Author

James Bernstein has been working with various companies in the IT field since 2000, managing technologies such as SAN and NAS storage, VMware, backups, Windows Servers, Active Directory, DNS, DHCP, Networking, Microsoft Office, Exchange, and more.

He has obtained certifications from Microsoft, VMware, CompTIA, ShoreTel, and SNIA, and continues to strive to learn new technologies to further his knowledge on a variety of subjects.

He is also the founder of the website onlinecomputertips.com, which offers its readers valuable information on topics such as Windows, networking, hardware, software, and troubleshooting. Jim writes much of the content himself, and adds new content on a regular basis. The site was started in 2005 and is still going strong today.

Index

A

B

C

D

Datacenter 30, 112
Datagram 13, 68
DCHP 53
Delimiter 14
DHCP 4, 11, 47, 50, 52, 67, 95, 132, 137
DHCPAck 53
DHCPDiscover 53
DHCPOffer 53
DHCPRequest 53
Displaydns 95
Distance vector 73
DNS 4, 11, 67
DoD 65, 79
Domain 9, 15, 80, 85, 88, 101, 108
Duplex 3, 32, 33
Dynamic 11, 52, 67, 70
Dynamic NAT 70

E

Echo 69, 96-98
EIGRP 74
Encryption 43, 44, 63, 67
Ethernet 3, 10, 24, 28, 100, 123
Ethernet Cables 24

F

Fiber optic cables 3, 10, 29, 126
Firewall 3, 5, 21, 90
Flushdns 95
FQDN 98, 105
Fragments 69
Frame 13, 14
Frames 3, 12, 13
FTP 21, 67
Full duplex 33

G

Gateway 4, 46, 76
GBIC 17
Gbps 11
Global unicast address 63

H

Half duplex 33
Handshake 44, 69
Header 14
Headers 3, 12, 14
Hexadecimal 62, 64
Hops 73
Host 11
Hostname 67
Http 66, 80
Https 67, 80, 141
Hub 3, 18
Hyper-V 115
Hypervisor 112, 114

I

IaaS 117
ICMP 69
IEEE 41
Ifconfig 50
IGMP 69
Inter-VLAN 60
Internet Layer Protocols 69
IP 69
IP address 11
IP addressing 45
ipconfig 5, 93, 137
IPsec 91
IPv6 61
ISO 12
ISP 11
IVR 60, 61

L

M

N

O

Overloading NAT 72
P

PaaS 117
Packet 11, 13
Pathping 98, 137
Peer to Peer 7
Ping 69, 90, 96-98, 133, 136, 137
Port 11
Preamble 14
Protocols 10 65

Q

QOS 64

R

Resolver cache 95
RFI 29
Ring 34
RIP 73
Rollover Cables 27
Router 3, 19, 46
Routes 72

S

SaaS 117
SAN 116
Shielding 24, 29
Simplex 3, 32, 33
Single Mode 30
SNMP 68
SSH 67
SSID 3, 40
SSL 67
Star topology 36
Static NAT 71
Subnets 21, 45, 60
Subnetting 4, 58

Made in the USA
Monee, IL
27 November 2019